Praise for *Because*

"Shannon Banks has defined the field of social leadership. From exemplifying great leadership at Microsoft to developing exceptional leaders across the globe, Shannon embodies what it means to be a social leader. *Because* translates her wisdom and experience into concrete, approachable steps, enabling and encouraging each of us to become more purpose-driven leaders. Every chapter delivers powerful insights and tools to lead more inclusive, innovative, and impactful teams."

—Matthew Kotler, partner group product manager at Microsoft

"*Because* is the best book on leadership that I have read in the past twenty years! Banks provides both powerful theory and clear, practical exercises to help the reader become a successful leader who knows 'why' as well as 'how' to lead."

—Michael Marquardt, professor emeritus at
George Washington University and cofounder
of World Institute for Action Learning

"*Because* is a powerful and galvanizing book that will take every leader on their own inspiring and important journey. Shannon brings to life the opportunity for and responsibility of leaders to create positive change not just with their teams and organizations but with communities and, indeed, the world at large. With practical tools and tangible examples, this book enables leaders to know themselves better and to step into being a social leader, crafting and living out their own personal purpose and leadership brand. This book is a must for leaders, and the impact of social leadership is a must for society—because if every leader was a social leader, the world would be a better place."

—Claire Fox, founder and managing director of Claire Fox
Coaching, former chief operating officer at UNICEF UK, and
author of *Work-Life Symbiosis: The Model for Happiness and Balance*

"Shannon Banks is an incredible professional whose work motivates and challenges top managers worldwide. With her skills and patience, she aims to help managers be authentic and connect their reason for working to their reason for living."

—Claudia Belli, head of financial inclusion and
relations with civil society at BNP Paribas

"It's one thing to be aware of the importance of strong connections, but it's quite another to cultivate them. In *Because*, Shannon Banks proposes a comprehensive yet pragmatic framework to help any leader or team turn that awareness into concrete actions. The improved connections bring better performance, motivation, and happiness."

—Peter Cauwelier, PhD, author and speaker, and Master Action
Learning Coach at World Institute for Action Learning, Thailand

"*Because* is a practical guide for anyone looking for meaning in life. Shannon Banks has beautifully blended concepts in a way that motivates the reader and inspires action."

—Dr. Usman Javaid, chief products and
marketing officer at Orange Business

"Shannon has perfected the art of combining inspiration and practicality with this book. Integrating the discussion of who we are as leaders with practical tools we can all use in our everyday work lives is just brilliant. A must read for any leader looking for their own 'why' and 'how' in order to create sustained impact."

—Angela McKenna, executive vice president of
EMEA employee success at Salesforce

"I love this book. It comes from a leader who lives what she writes. *Because* is as profound as it is practical. It triggers a lot of introspection but then walks you through reflections and offers tips that give the deep thinking a concrete direction. It is also incredibly timely, providing a much-needed reshaping of leadership for a transforming world."

—Tony Crabbe, business psychologist and author
of *Busy: How to Thrive in a World of Too Much*

Because

Because

12 Essential Skills for Connecting How You Lead with Why

Shannon Banks

BE

Published by Be Studios, London

www.shannonbanksauthor.com

GIRL FRIDAY
PRODUCTIONS

Edited and designed by Girl Friday Productions

www.girlfridayproductions.com

Design: Zach Hooker

Project management: Sara Addicott and Laura Dailey

Image credits: © Shannon Banks, Yeshi Kangrang/Unsplash, Levi XU/Unsplash, Jamie Street/Unsplash, Death to Stock, Shannon Banks, Pexels/Pixabay, Markus/Unsplash, Angus Grey/Unsplash, Khyta/Unsplash, Tim Swaan/Unsplash

ISBN (hardcover): 978-1-7394246-2-6

ISBN (paperback): 978-1-7394246-0-2

ISBN (ebook): 978-1-7394246-1-9

First edition

Contents

Introduction

B efore I tell you why I wrote this book, I want to start with its name.

I love words. As a young child, I read my way through playtime and recess, and I dreamed of being an editor. I borrowed my mother's typewriter and created my own newsletters. Eventually, I studied journalism at university and spent some time working in magazine publishing.

As much as I loved words, I realized I loved people more, so I put the pen to one side and meandered my way through the corporate world, each step taking me closer and closer to my real purpose: working with people to help them be the best leaders they can be.

But this passion for words has never really dissipated, so naming my company, and naming my book, have been personal, carefully considered decisions.

My company is called Be Leadership. We help organizations bring their social purpose to life through their people. We provide experiences that develop exceptional *social leaders*—leaders who not only have a strong business impact but think beyond the business to broader society. My company name includes the word *be* because I am a believer that both business and social impact start with true human-centered behaviors. The development of a more successful organization can start with just one individual—one who is clear on their purpose, or reason to be, and brings this to life in their daily work by being authentic, inspiring, collaborative, and inclusive. *Being*.

That's where this book comes in. For you to be a good leader today, it is imperative that you consider the impact you have on the world as well as on the people around you. Leadership requires that you think about not only what you do but how you do it. And you need to live and lead in alignment with your greater purpose. This book is here to help you do that.

My Crooked Path to Greater Purpose

So why the title *Because*? The etymology of the word *because* is a blend of Middle English *by cause* and Old French *par cause de* or *by reason of*. It's a perfect mix of *be*—the human-centered behavior I mentioned—and *cause*, which can be both what gives rise to action as well as something worth defending. It is also the answer to the questions of how and why you lead. The skills and behaviors make up the *how* of your leadership, and the cause you are committed to is the *why*. Reading this book will help you bring these two leadership dimensions together to become a stronger social leader, increasing your impact and helping you live a life of greater purpose.

Sometimes finding this purpose isn't straightforward. Our careers can take what Mary Klayder, associate director of undergraduate studies at the University of Kansas, likes to call a "crooked path."[1] My crooked path led me to where I am today and helped me develop my passion around this work. It started more than twenty-five years ago when I was working as a leader at Microsoft. I was a group program manager, in charge of a large team of people designing the user experience for a new product. I loved coaching my team and the intellectual problems we were solving. I was recognized as a strong manager and got great feedback from my employees. I enjoyed the creativity inherent in the role. But I had fallen accidentally into a career in software, and I felt some level of dissatisfaction that I couldn't put a name to. So while I had a clear career mapped out ahead of me, I found myself making decisions that took me on a different road altogether.

I moved to England and became the international product planning lead for Microsoft Office, heading a worldwide team in performing customer research to help make decisions around the development of the product. Again—a great role with huge impact: helping to shape a business with $8 billion in annual sales and more than 450 million users. But after a few years, I left on maternity leave, and when I came back, I moved a step closer to what I really love. After nearly a decade of working on software with people alongside me, I wanted to move people to the center. I took a job in leadership development.

It was in this role that I found my purpose, or what I like to call my *reason to be*: I moved closer to my strengths and spent my days designing large-scale global programs that helped leaders accelerate their development and increase their impact. And it was in this position that I discovered my passion for what I now call *social leadership* and designed an award-winning program that brought together learning, positive impact, and business results through work with nonprofit partners in the developing world. I took this love for social leadership into my work when I eventually left Microsoft to start a company of my own.

At Be Leadership, we work with leaders to help them identify and articulate their own reason to be. We have worked with thousands of leaders using the social leadership framework I introduce in this book, coaching them to develop these skills and increase their impact. As research for this book, I analyzed the data from more than six hundred leaders who have completed our online social leadership self-assessment. Alongside this, I interviewed a range of leaders whom I see as exemplars, people who bring these skills and behaviors to life every day and are living and working in alignment with their purpose. This book is intended as a resource to support you in doing this yourself.

What to Expect

This is more than just a book. It is a tool kit of exercises that help you reflect on your individual purpose and how you can foster that in your personal and professional life through twelve skills that make up the foundation of the social leadership framework. These skills are being courageous, authentic, flexible, curious, inclusive, resourceful, transparent, collaborative, present, accountable, giving, and inspiring.

The exercises designed around strengthening these twelve social leadership skills are ones you can take off the page and start practicing right now. Every chapter also concludes with a Take Action section with even more tips and actionable items to help you apply what you're learning.

While most of the exercises you'll find in the chapters are meant for self-study and self-reflection, I haven't forgotten about your teams. In the back, you will also find a set of group exercises, one structured around the theme of each chapter. Once you feel you have a foundation in the skills discussed, you can use these group exercises to strengthen your skills and foster them in your team too.

Along the way, I also include reflection questions that help you dig deeper. I recommend you spend some time journaling around these questions as they come up in your reading. You might consider purchasing a special notebook that you dedicate to your learning journey.

Alongside this, you might write reflections on sticky notes and put them on your wall, computer monitor, or mirror. You might contemplate them as you take a morning walk or commute to the office. Whatever you decide, I encourage you to find ways to make them work for you. I will give you some advice on what has worked for my clients and me, but you should feel free to adapt them so you can incorporate them into your day-to-day life.

Finally, if you want even more resources to support your social leadership development, you can visit shannonbanksauthor.com, where I link to free online tools and offer fresh, updated content to support you in your learning.

By the time you reach the end of this book, you will have crafted a purpose statement that encapsulates your reason to be across both your personal and your professional lives. You will use this as the foundation for your leadership brand. If you know your purpose and can articulate it clearly, it will help you to make better decisions and lead more effectively. But before we get there, let's break down what we'll be exploring in each chapter.

Chapter 1 sets the context for why social leadership skills matter and lays out societal changes that impact the way we live and lead today. These changes, which include the need to remain human-centric in an increasingly technology-driven world and the importance of placing a growing emphasis on purpose and responsible leadership, are shaping our world in significant ways. The skills we focus on are those most needed within this context.

In chapter 2, I share a set of practical exercises you can work through to help you find clarity on your reason to be. These exercises, which explore your strengths, values, and areas of true passion, provide a foundation for the rest of our work together.

Chapters 3 through 8 look at the twelve social leadership skills in combinations of two. Focusing on these skills will accelerate your leadership development and help you increase your effectiveness. While I look at these largely through the lens of a workplace, I believe all of us need these skills, and I aim to ensure these chapters are helpful whether or not you are in paid employment.

Finally, in chapter 9, I return to your purpose and look at what you want to be known for as a leader.

Chapter Title	Focus and Skills	Why This Is Important
Chapter 1: **Social Leadership in Practice**	Exploring societal changes	Because the world is changing and so should your leadership
Chapter 2: **Exploring Your Reason to Be**	Understanding your purpose	Because reflecting on your values, passions, and strengths can help you discover your purpose
Chapter 3: **Leading with Courageous Authenticity**	Being courageous and authentic	Because the courage to be authentic is the foundation for deeper relationships
Chapter 4: **Adopting a Beginner's Mindset**	Being flexible and curious	Because by keeping an open mind, you can move beyond your limiting beliefs
Chapter 5: **Harnessing Diverse Thinking**	Being inclusive and resourceful	Because being inclusive and overcoming bias can help us be more innovative
Chapter 6: **Building Teams That Talk**	Being transparent and collaborative	Because transparency is a foundation for effective collaboration
Chapter 7: **Focusing on Accountability**	Being present and accountable	Because focusing on what matters most increases accountability
Chapter 8: **Leading by Example**	Being giving and inspiring	Because we are more inspiring when we give back and show others the way
Chapter 9: **Building Your Leadership Brand**	Appreciating your impact	Because we all have an impact

I know from my own personal leadership journey that when we make choices that are aligned with our own *because*, it leads to greater happiness, more energy, better well-being, and a more positive impact on the world around us. And that's what I wish for you.

This book will help you become stronger, more impactful, and more purposeful. It will help you lead in a way that positively impacts those around you, the organizations you are part of, and your broader community. Good luck, and thanks for your commitment to this experience.

Chapter 1

Social Leadership in Practice

Because the world is changing and so should your leadership

What impact do you have on the people around you?

"*You cannot get through a single day without having an impact on the world around you. What you do makes a difference, and you have to decide what kind of difference you want to make.*"

— Jane Goodall, English primatologist

E very one of us has an impact. It can be positive or negative, limited or world changing. The impact you have may not be obvious in the moment. You may feel what you are doing and who you are aren't making a huge difference. Nonetheless, the choices we make and the way we live—and the way we lead—matter.

You may be an entrepreneur, a team leader at a start-up, a parent volunteer, or a CEO in a multinational company. You may be a tenured leader with a track record of success or a recent graduate exploring new career paths. You may or may not consider yourself to be a leader. But this book is for you. Leadership is not dependent on a role, position, or title; instead, it is a mindset. We choose how we lead ourselves and those around us with every decision we make. To be a social leader means extending this view to consider how your decisions impact the broader community around you.

Leadership is not dependent on a role, position, or title; instead, it is a mindset. We choose how we lead ourselves and those around us with every decision we make.

Social leadership has two dimensions: The first is a mindset around social impact and clarity around why positive impact matters. The second is having the skills and behaviors needed to support that shift and maximize a leader's success in today's work environment. I believe that with an expanded perspective, the right skills, and greater self-awareness, each of us has the ability to lead in a way that inspires others to greatness.

I want you to become crystal clear around your purpose and develop the leadership behaviors that will help you succeed in living it. To do this, we will start by exploring what matters most in our lives, reflecting on our strengths, values, and passions and how they come together to shape the people we are. Then we'll look more in depth at the twelve skills needed for success in the modern world by considering these questions:

1 What leadership skills do we most need, and how can we practice them in our daily lives?

2 What do our leadership strengths tell us about our greater purpose and leadership brand?

3 How might we use what we've learned to expand our perspectives and increase our effectiveness?

The twelve skills we are covering in chapters 3 through 8 were selected based on societal and behavioral trends that started emerging more than two decades ago and have been amplified by the global events of recent years. Before we get into exploring the skills, let's spend this chapter focusing on two changes that are required based on these trends, ones that I feel will continue to shape the way we lead and work for years to come.

Change 1: The Need to Remain Human-Centered in a Technology-Driven World

Reflection: Think back to January 2020. How was life different? Now think about the present. How well are you dealing with the uncertainty and pace of the world today?

I was an employee at Microsoft for more than seventeen years. When I joined, I worked from its headquarters in Redmond, Washington, but midway through my career there, I took a position in England. After that move, I had a series of globally distanced managers and team members, and we relied heavily on conference calls, email, and other technology to collaborate. During that time, I even had one manager I never met in person: he hired me based on phone interviews, and we worked together for nearly a year before he moved on to a new role.

At the time, this virtual collaboration was something foreign to many of my colleagues and friends. I got so used to online meetings, it became my default—when people suggested we meet, I assumed first they meant virtually and was surprised when they expected me to get on a train or airplane. But this has all changed in the past few years. Let's take a look at the major shifts and how we can positively navigate them.

24/7 Connectivity and Hybrid Working

As in other times of crisis, our experience finding our way through COVID-19 led to rapid innovation.[2] Whether it's a pandemic, a war, or another natural catastrophe, crises demand immediate response. As people and organizations, we become more courageous during a crisis as we balance our decisions against the risk of not acting. Suddenly, what seemed impossible becomes achievable. During the pandemic, this led to dramatic behavioral change and technology adoption: Families started using online conferencing platforms like Zoom, WhatsApp, and FaceTime to stay connected. We even started holding online funerals, baby showers, and game nights.

In the workplace, companies jumped forward in their videoconferencing use, moving everything from one-to-one meetings to large-scale events online. As one of the leading conferencing platforms, Zoom saw annual meetings increase 3,300 percent year over year between early 2020 and early 2021, and in 2020, they had 485 million downloads of their mobile app.[3] As a society and as individuals, we increased our capacity and creativity around what was possible for distanced collaboration.

There are unquestionable advantages to having this technology in our lives. On a personal level, I recognize this: technology allows me, an American who has spent more than twenty years living in Europe, to stay in contact with colleagues, family, and friends around the world. We benefit as business leaders too—we are more able to communicate with customers and clients, stakeholders, and a distributed workforce. We can learn about critical issues twenty-four hours a day, seven days a week, allowing us to react more quickly from anywhere. The connectivity afforded by technology allows for flexible working, faster information sharing, and efficiency.

But this constant connectivity also creates its own challenges. In my work with clients, I hear repeated concerns around work-life balance, exhaustion, and an extended workday—challenges exacerbated by technology. Studies run since 2020 have shown that our average workday has increased in recent years, with us working at least 8 percent, or forty-five minutes, more every day.[4] These same studies show that we are spending more time working late into the evening, attending more meetings, and working on the weekends.

This has left us feeling tired. During the past few years, my clients have reported feeling overworked and have struggled with work-life balance. It's not uncommon for people to say they are exhausted by the strain of managing too many priorities and a longer workday. We struggle with being always on, juggling the many dimensions of our lives, and working too many hours. From my own experience, I know the combination of managing a family and home life plus working with a global team and clients that span time zones leaves very little time for rest and well-being.

Remote working leaves us feeling more isolated too. In a recent study, one-third of people reported feeling lonely when working online.[5] While working from home saves us time sitting behind the wheel or on a train commuting to the office and gives us some independent time to focus on longer tasks, it doesn't allow for the hallway conversations and watercooler chats that make our work life rich. All of this impacts our well-being and ultimately saps our productivity and effectiveness.

Whatever the pros and cons, hybrid, flexible working is here to stay. While many people want to return to the office, an equal number want the ability to work from home. Most studies conclude that we will need to support a certain amount of flexibility moving forward.[6] Therefore, we need to figure out how to manage this in a good way.

A Way Back to Connection

If you are working in an environment that is facing the challenges I just described, here's how you can be most effective: your impact is dependent on your ability to move from connectivity to connection. This is not about how much time you are spending in meetings or on devices or how busy you are. It's about creating real relationships.

Connection is essential to life satisfaction. A key piece of research around this is the Harvard Study of Adult Development, which was released widely for the first time in 2014. It's an ongoing longitudinal study looking at what makes us happy. In this study, researchers followed people for more than seventy-five years and explored what brought them joy. They had five key findings, two of which relate directly to connection and relationships.[7]

The first thing they found was that love is the foundation for happiness. They summed this up: "Happiness is love. Full stop." While this is a powerful statement, you might be asking how it is relevant to your work. This is where the second finding comes in: the broader and richer the relationships in our lives, the better, and having a wide range of deep relationships with people is the strongest predictor of life satisfaction. So this connection that we have with others is essential to our happiness. And if we go one step further, if we're happy

Your impact is dependent on your ability to move from connectivity to connection. This is not about how much time you are spending in meetings or on devices or how busy you are. It's about creating real relationships.

at work, we are more motivated and more productive not only at work but in all areas of life.

Everyone may believe this in theory, but creating these deep connections at work is easier said than done. When you take a bunch of tired, overworked, and isolated individuals and put them together on a team, it's not particularly conducive to team building. One study found that 86 percent of virtual teams struggled with building relationships.[8] To create real connections in a virtual or hybrid environment requires concerted, ongoing effort. Unfortunately, when time is tight and people are tired, this focus on human interaction can be the first thing to go. According to the Microsoft Work Trend Index report, leaders need to make a commitment to finding time and space for deepening relationships beyond the transactional. "When work-life balance is out of whack, most people cut out relationship building for more urgent matters," said Constance Noonan Hadley, an organizational psychologist who studies workplace relationships. "Regardless of remote status, building relationships will still feel like a luxury workers cannot afford unless there is a shift in how time is prioritized and valued by managers."[9]

Fostering Learning Agility

One of the reasons the day may feel too short to spend needed time on relationships is we are facing an unprecedented pace of change in our work and home lives, and we are bombarded by an overwhelming amount of data and information.[10] From the moment we wake up, we are blasted with information from Facebook, TikTok, news channels, podcasts, YouTube videos, email, and Slack, not to mention television (and the countless streaming services on offer), radio, and other traditional news sources. In large part due to big data and automation, the amount of data generated is growing at an exponential rate, with 90 percent being generated in the past two years alone.[11]

On top of this, we must learn to use new products, deal with unprecedented situations, and get our heads around emerging technologies. Take the example of OpenAI's ChatGPT, the artificial intelligence (AI) bot that responds to chat queries with humanlike answers: Within one week of its launch in late 2022, ChatGPT was reported to have reached more than one million users.[12] This grew to 100 million active monthly users by early the following year, making it one of the fastest growing consumer applications in history.[13] Companies everywhere started thinking through what impact this could have on their business.

Taking this all in and making sense of what's happening in the world can feel overwhelming. Within the workplace, we need to learn to deal with this by developing new skills in data-driven decision-making, critical analysis, and storytelling. Across our lives, we need the ability to question the data we have and consider its biases. With the amount of data that is produced today, it is essential that we understand our priorities and values and can determine what data we need to allow us to thrive as leaders and social organizations.

All of this change has an impact on jobs and skills. With these rapid advances, the World Economic Forum anticipated that 65 percent of kids who are in school today will, when they graduate, hold jobs that don't yet exist.[14] What this means is that in a decade, not only will some jobs be irrelevant in the face of technology, but new roles will be created, roles that—given the right skills and capabilities—we can take on and within which we can be successful.

Success is dependent on our learning agility—our ability to be adaptable and move flexibly into these new domains. Effective social leaders must increasingly supplement their industry and functional expertise with a general capacity for learning, and they must develop that capacity in the people they supervise.

From Content Expertise to Context Leadership

I like to talk about this adjustment as moving from content expertise to context leadership. In days past, you could learn something, and once you learned it, the world was slow enough that the information remained relevant for the next twenty to thirty years. You could largely rely on that knowledge for your decision-making, confident that your status and credibility would remain intact. Today, there's lots of information available, and the world is changing quickly, so while it's still important, subject matter expertise is no longer enough.

As a leader, especially as you grow more and more senior, instead of leading from the front, you have to be able to set context for other people so they can work efficiently and effectively without you. And at the same time, you need to retain enough context yourself that you can step in and inspect to move things along and help unblock decisions when needed.

Chantal Peyre De Fabregues invests a lot of time making sure those on her team have the context they need to be successful.[15] As head of leadership development and change management at the international banking group BNP Paribas, Peyre De Fabregues looks for opportunities to share leadership with her team members and creates clear ownership for new initiatives. "We onboard the whole team around new initiatives whether they are personally involved or not," she said. "We spend time during our weekly meetings to make sure the context is shared across the group."

Peyre De Fabregues also gives her team members the opportunity to experience for themselves what they are offering to other teams in the organization. This ensures deeper awareness of the programs being developed as well as learning from direct experience. She added to her earlier comments, "We created a workshop for teams and managers to define their sustainability mission, and we are going to test this as a team ourselves. We will explore how we contribute to sustainability and create a team purpose that aligns with both the purpose of the company and our personal purpose."

In our fast-paced, technology-driven environment, we need leaders like Peyre De Fabregues who work alongside others and provide the context needed for meaningful connections and better decision-making. If we rely on one person, in a hierarchical command-and-control structure, it's too slow and rigid for the modern world. Efficiency is not the same as effectiveness. We need to lead from the middle.

Taken together, these shifts introduced by the growing reliance on technology make it even more essential that we focus on the skills that differentiate us as humans. Our abilities to think critically, be flexible, and work together to solve problems all become more important, as do the skills that help us connect with one another and form real relationships. Technology doesn't take away the demand for good leadership; it amplifies it.

Change 2: The Need to Place Greater Emphasis on Purpose and Responsible Leadership

Reflection: When you think about positive impact and responsible leadership, what companies and organizations come to mind for you? How does their reputation influence your relationship with these businesses?

The second trend that creates a framework for this book is around the growing importance of purpose and responsibility in business. If you look back about fifty years, social leadership didn't matter to most companies or leaders. In fact, Milton Friedman, a well-respected economist, voiced and documented what a lot of people felt at that time, which was that the only social responsibility of a business was

If we rely on one person, in a hierarchical command-and-control structure, it's too slow and rigid for the modern world. Efficiency is not the same as effectiveness.

to increase profit. In his often-quoted Friedman doctrine, published in the *New York Times* in 1970, he wrote, "There is one and only one social responsibility of business—to use its resources and engage in activities designed to increase its profits so long as it stays within the rules of the game, which is to say, engages in open and free competition without deception or fraud."[16]

Purpose and Shared Value

While that profit-only view may have been prevalent then, it thankfully isn't any longer. Today, business leaders and organizations are more likely to recognize the concept of what we call *shared value*—creating economic value while addressing social needs and challenges. As early as 2011, Michael Porter and Mark Kramer wrote in *Harvard Business Review*, "Shared value is not social responsibility, philanthropy, or even sustainability, but a new way to achieve economic success."[17]

A lot of evidence backs this up: Research by John Kotter and James Heskett showed that over a decade-long period, purposeful, value-driven companies outperformed their counterparts in stock price by a factor of twelve.[18] Another study found purpose-driven companies outperformed the Standard and Poor's 500 (S&P 500) by ten times over a fifteen-year period. And since that time, a focus on purpose and positive impact has exploded. In 2011, just 20 percent of S&P 500 companies published reports on corporate social responsibility and related initiatives; by 2018, that figure had risen to 86 percent.[19] Today that number exceeds 95 percent.[20]

In a recent study, 82 percent of employees affirmed the importance of purpose, but only 42 percent felt their company's stated "purpose" had much effect.[21] The British Academy agreed there's a need to develop a new contract between business and society, where businesses "profitably solve the problems of people and planet, and not profit from creating problems."[22]

You might wonder why all this focus on purpose. There are a number of reasons, ranging from a shift in societal values to a forced response to public scrutiny. However, we shouldn't underestimate the positive business case:

- A focus on positive impact and social purpose positively affects brand reputation—When done well and authentically, strategic corporate social responsibility impacts products, culture, and the balance sheet.

- This helps with recruiting and retention—A company's purpose is especially important to Millennials and Gen Zs, with research indicating that these employees frequently consider a company's social commitments when choosing where to work.[23]

- This in turn has an impact on employee engagement—In a recent Harvard Business Review executive study, 89 percent of people said companies with shared purpose would have greater employee satisfaction.[24]

- Finally, societal events in recent years bring this into focus— War, the pandemic, and social unrest have reminded us that people are motivated at the highest levels when they can connect their work contributions to a greater purpose and mission. As employees, we care about the stance of our companies on these societal-level events.

Responsible Leadership

You may recognize this shift to purpose within the organization you work for: Are its purpose, vision, and mission clear? Is the purpose lived in the behaviors of the leaders? Do you see it reinforced in the workplace? Hopefully you do.

Some organizations have their purpose at their very core. In these companies, purpose is reflected across the organization's experience —from strategy to operations, and from people to product. One such company is Marco Polo, a video chat application whose purpose is "helping people feel close." CEO and cofounder Vlada Bortnik described the creation of Marco Polo's purpose as the most important decision she and her cofounder and husband Michal made for the company.[25]

Instead of starting with a business opportunity, she said they had a conversation around what they wanted for their family. "We started reading everything we could about happiness research because we wanted more happiness for our kids," Bortnik said. "And we were perhaps brazen enough to think that if we just learned about it, we could make it happen."

Bortnik's research highlighted how important relationships are for happiness, and with their own extended families living thousands of miles away, they knew how difficult it was to have meaningful contact. This led them to their purpose, and Marco Polo was born.

Today, Bortnik said the company's purpose impacts the company "in a thousand different ways." From investors to board meetings, hiring to pitches, product features to employee engagement, the purpose is front and center. "I can't think of any important decision we make that isn't impacted by our purpose," she said.

If you work for an organization like Marco Polo with a clear purpose, there's value in finding points of alignment between your personal reason to be and your organization's mission. If you don't work within this context, clarity around your individual purpose will help you make better decisions around where to invest your time and possibly even what companies to work for in the future.

The start of the pandemic made many of us reconsider our reason to be and the values we hold. It led many people to change roles and focus on new activities. Around the world, we saw a so-called Great Resignation—or Great Attrition—with employees voluntarily leaving the workforce in large numbers. While there is much debate around all the forces behind this, many agree that one way to combat this trend is to invest more in the human aspects of work. As leaders, if we are clear on our purpose and are working in alignment with it, we bring greater satisfaction, productivity, and higher levels of well-being to everyone.

To be effective leaders in today's environment, we need to consider the impact we have on the world as well as on the people around us. Being a true social leader requires a demonstrated ability to think beyond the business to broader society. As leaders, we must think not only about what we do but how and why we do it.

To be effective leaders in today's environment, we need to consider the impact we have on the world as well as on the people around us.

Take Action

The societal trends and changes covered in this chapter influence the way we live and the leadership we need to provide. Before we explore the twelve social leadership skills in the coming chapters, it's useful to think about how these societal changes are impacting you directly. Take some time to reflect on this influence using the following prompts:

1 *Perform a technology audit*—Make a list of all the applications and devices you use in your work and personal life. How do you currently feel about the amount of connectivity you have? How connected are you with others? Where does technology help, and where does it hinder?

2 *Consider technology's impact on you*—Think about how technology has changed your profession and life in the last ten years, five years, and two years. If you project forward five years, what changes can you imagine, and how do you feel about them?

3 *Reconnect*—We know from the Harvard study that the richer and deeper our connections, the happier we are. Reflect on the close relationships in your life. How connected do you feel? Consider reaching out to properly reconnect with at least one person.

4 *Check your reliance on subject matter expertise*—Reflect on your areas of expertise and how dependent you are on these for status and credibility. How able are you to flex into new domains as they emerge? How confident do you feel sharing your knowledge and leadership with others?

5 *Find areas of alignment*—Think back on any organizations you've worked for. Have you been aware of purpose statements for any of these companies? How have they demonstrated (or not demonstrated) their commitment to that statement? How aligned have your views been to their vison and mission?

In the next chapter, we will turn the focus inward to help you discover and proudly articulate your personal purpose.

Chapter 2

Exploring Your Reason to Be

Because reflecting on your values, passions, and strengths can help you discover your purpose

REFLECTION

What experiences have you had that allowed you to see things from a new perspective? What impact did that have on your life?

*"Find out who you are and
do it on purpose."*

—Dolly Parton, American singer-songwriter

I grew up in Midwest America with parents who were both service oriented and globally minded. From early on in my childhood, they opened our home to others. Foster children, exchange students, and extended family joined us for months or sometimes years, adding richness and perspective to our lives. When I was sixteen, I was given the opportunity to experience this in reverse—I flew to Finland to live with one of the families we had made part of our own. That perspective-building year ignited a lifelong passion for experiential learning.

This early opportunity gave me the confidence and appetite for further travel. In 1992, when I was twenty-one, I had the chance to study abroad, so I moved to Saint Petersburg, Russia, as part of my undergraduate education. It was just after the collapse of the Soviet Union, and it was hard. Food was in shortage because workers had walked away from the communal farms, and all the crops were rotting in the fields. It was spring, and hungry ice fishermen were drowning and floating ashore after fishing when the ice was too thin. We had Russian roommates who were disillusioned. As American university students, we were millionaires compared to our friends, but it didn't matter as there was nothing to buy. We had to search through empty supermarkets, just like our Russian friends.

One day my roommate got sick—really sick, with a serious infection. I thought she needed some vitamin C, so I went to the Beryozka, which was a black market hard-currency store, most often frequented by the Russian mafia or tourists. I found a liter of orange juice there for about twenty dollars and was standing in line to buy it. In front of me, a middle-aged American woman was looking for matches. She had come to Russia to see the palaces, she told the Russian man at the checkout. She had run out of matches and wanted a cigarette. Being the kind of store it was, the Beryozka didn't have any matches.

I, the twenty-one-year-old American with my OJ, was behind her. I said, "I saw some matches this morning in the Russian supermarket across the street. I am a student here. I can take you over there and help you buy them." She said, "Oh great! I'd like to get some fruit too." I shook my head with skepticism. "You won't find any fruit there, I'm afraid. It's a Russian store, and there is a shortage of everything. It's pretty empty. But I did see matches, and it would give you a chance to see what it's really like living here at the moment."

There is benefit in seeing the world through a new lens, stepping—or sometimes even being pushed—out of our comfort zone.

"Oh no," she said, shrinking back. "I don't think I want to do that. I came to see the palaces." She left without her matches and without the broader perspective on what it was really like to be in Russia.

This experience solidified for me the value of being open to different perspectives. There is benefit in seeing the world through a new lens, stepping—or sometimes even being pushed—out of our comfort zone.

As the years passed and I entered the world of work, I made it a mission to help people develop new perspectives, and I worked to ensure I created this challenge for myself in every role I took. I discovered over years of doing this for myself and others that when you constantly stretch yourself in these ways, you can make a greater impact. The first step is defining your purpose. In this chapter, I will guide you through a few simple exercises to help you make a start on this.

Why Purpose Matters

Each one of us has a purpose—a core mission or reason for being that is central to our life. When we know and can express our purpose, it creates meaning; helps guide our goals, behaviors, and decisions; and offers us a sense of direction. People who discover their purpose in life know who they are, what they are, and why they are. And when we know ourselves, it becomes easier to live a life of integrity and authenticity.

Over the course of a life, an average person will spend ninety-two thousand hours at work.[26] For life fulfillment, it's important that this time be spent on something that gives you meaning. It's better for both you and your employer if you're working in alignment with your purpose or reason to be. As author James Kerr wrote in *Legacy*, where he analyzes the culture of the All Blacks rugby team, "Personal meaning is the way we connect to a wider team purpose. If our values and beliefs are aligned with the values and beliefs of the organization, then we will work harder towards its success. If not, our individual motivation and purpose will suffer, and so will the organization."[27]

According to recent research, people who live their purpose at work are healthier, more productive, and more resilient than people who don't.[28] They are also more likely to stay at the company.[29] When the purpose of employees and the organization are aligned, the benefits to the company expand even further to include stronger engagement and commitment, deeper loyalty, and a greater willingness to recommend their company to others.

People who discover their purpose in life know who they are, what they are, and why they are. And when we know ourselves, it becomes easier to live a life of integrity and authenticity.

Today only about 20 to 25 percent of adults claim to have clarity around their individual purpose,[30] and even fewer can explain their purpose to others.[31] When we achieve this clarity, the resulting self-awareness can make us better at our jobs, better communicators, and more confident. In fact, research has shown that self-awareness is the strongest predictor of leadership success,[32] and clearer purpose may lead to greater well-being, reduced feelings of loneliness, and a stronger sense of personal direction.[33]

Three elements can help form your individual purpose:

1 Values

2 Passions

3 Strengths

By getting clarity around each of these, you will be more prepared to develop a purpose statement that encapsulates your reason to be across the personal and professional. This will bring you clarity around the unique contributions you make in life—contributions that form part of your leadership brand and legacy. Let's take a look at these three elements and how they can help you gain clarity about your purpose and put it into practice as a social leader.

*Knowing our values,
even when we're not
able to live and behave
completely in alignment
with them, allows us to
know ourselves.*

Discovering Your Values

Reflection: What motivates you to go to work each day?

A core component of our purpose is our value system. Values aren't something that we talk about a lot, but they really guide our behavior. They are our basic and fundamental beliefs that drive or motivate our actions. They help us determine what's important to us. Knowing our values, even when we're not able to live and behave completely in alignment with them, allows us to know ourselves. They are essential for self-awareness.

Getting clarity around our true values can be challenging. Values are often shaped in our early life by our parents, families, siblings, family history, education, and friends. In these early years, we create stories about who we are and how we should be in the world. We decide what we need to do to fit in, be accepted, and be loved. These so-called *conditions of worth* can drive our behavior into adulthood, and they can sometimes cause us to associate ourselves with values that have come from self-limiting beliefs or assumptions.

I recognize this from my own upbringing: I was raised by parents who were hugely supportive. I was taught from a very young age that I was smart and could achieve anything. This was motivating for me, and it encouraged me to take on big challenges and aim my sights high. It gave me confidence to achieve more. But like many people who have supportive parents, I found that some part of me started to believe that I *had* to exceed expectations. My condition of worth was around excelling. Some part of me began to believe that if I didn't get the highest grades or win the competitions or surpass my past achievements, I wasn't good enough. And my values as a young person, which included achievement, reflected this.

Once our values are defined, they start to impact the decisions we make. Being aware of them is important not only because they can guide us to make good decisions but also because they can create *unconscious bias*: when we make decisions based on our values and we aren't aware of it, we might judge other people from this basis, which can create prejudice.

Even if you think you know your values clearly, it can be worthwhile revisiting them and challenging yourself around how you are living them. Values are measures that we use to tell us if our life is turning out well. Living in alignment with our values brings contentment and happiness. But when things are out of alignment, we feel unsettled and dissatisfied. This is why it's important to get clarity on your values and also why they play a key role in understanding your purpose.

Remember that while there may be overlap, your values are different from your strengths (which we will look at later in this chapter). Often, we find it easier to identify our core values when we consider the people we most respect and reflect on why we admire them. We also can see our core values at play through experiences we find difficult or unsettling. This can be an indicator that our values are being challenged.

Reflecting on Values

Before getting into the next exercise, which will help you name your top values, spend some time brainstorming or journaling about what values you are currently leaning on day to day. Consider these questions:

- Whom do you most admire in your daily life? What is it about who they are that you respect?

- Who are your role models or mentors? What is it that they stand for that might be aligned with your values?

- Who are the people you see in the media or on social media whom you really don't like? What is it about them that bothers you? What might this say about your value system?

- When have you felt uncomfortable with a decision that you've made? When have you been involved in a conflict or a discussion where you haven't been true to yourself? Why did this matter, and to what value does it relate?

FAMILY	BALANCE	COURAGE	HEALTH	PRESENCE
ACCOUNTABILITY	RESOURCEFULNESS	GROWTH	CREATIVITY	TRUTH
INTEGRITY	BEAUTY	INSPIRATION	JUSTICE	INCLUSION
TRANSPARENCY	RECOGNITION	LOYALTY	SOLITUDE	HAPPINESS
HUMOR	WISDOM	BELONGING	ADVENTURE	SECURITY
EQUALITY	GIVING	RESILIENCE	FLEXIBILITY	EMPATHY
KNOWLEDGE	CONNECTION	LEARNING	MASTERY	PROSPERITY
AUTHENTICITY	CHALLENGE	CURIOSITY	ACHIEVEMENT	COLLABORATION
SPIRITUALITY	OPTIMISM	STRENGTH	FREEDOM	TRANQUILITY
REFLECTION	COMPETITION	INNOVATION	STRUCTURE	INDEPENDENCE

Top Three Values

While it's not uncommon to feel a connection to many values, there is benefit in narrowing your list to just a handful. Follow these steps to gain clarity on your top three:

1 Take a look at the list above, which is a compilation of values that are frequently identified by human beings across cultures.

2 Sort these values into three categories—high, medium, and low—based on their relative importance in your life. It may seem that every value is important to you, but try to use all three categories and think about them in relation to one another. If one of your values isn't here, then feel free to add it in your own words. It's important when selecting your values that you use words that mean something to you.

3 It's possible to have quite a few values, but probably there are just a few that guide most of your day-to-day life. So once you have created your priorities, take those in the high-priority category and sort them again, narrowing them down until you get to three that are most essential to your life satisfaction.

4 You might struggle to get down to your top three values. If that's the case, see if you have a few that relate to each other. One leader I worked with had family, humor, and spirituality all on his list as important values, but then decided he could summarize all of those with the word optimism, which really resonated for him.

Identifying Your Passions

As a next step in exploring your reason to be, it's helpful to identify your passions. If our values are our underlying beliefs, our passions are what we do when given full freedom of choice. Or, as American monk Thomas Merton once wrote, "The things that we love tell us what we are."[34]

When looking at passions, start by thinking about what projects or activities you have boundless energy for. These should be interests, hobbies, or pastimes that you love. Instead of sapping your strength, these activities usually bring you energy.

Reflection: When you have free time available, where and how do you choose to spend it? Why do you love spending time on these activities?

It's important to remember that these projects aren't what you feel you *should* do—they are what you actually make time for. Personally, I have a long list of "should dos." Some of these sound fun to me, at least in theory—studying more foreign languages, reading the complete history of Britain, finishing the embroidery project I started when my daughter was born. But when I have a free evening or am off work on vacation and get a chance to choose, I don't prioritize these shoulds.

Instead, I go running outdoors, volunteer in the town where I live, and weed my vegetable garden. These are my real passion projects, or what I refer to as *what-I-love activities*.

Usually certain themes connect these activities if we look deeply enough. On the surface, my what-I-love activities seem unrelated to one another. But when I reflect on why I love them, I see clear connections that pull them together. These connections or underlying themes are what really matter in helping us understand our purpose —they are our true passions.

For example, many of my favorite projects relate to social activity: a sense of community with other runners, producing food to share in my vegetable garden, sharing photography from travel with my family. All of these come together under the theme of "sharing." Similarly, several of the activities I love are related to my health: running makes me feel stronger and improves my fitness while vegetable gardening is physically satisfying; both fall under the theme of "strength." These umbrella terms—sharing and strength—are my *passions*, and when I am doing work that relates to these in some way, I feel more energized.

Leaders I have worked with have shared a broad range of activities relating to everything from traveling by camper van and mastering tae kwon do to learning a new violin tune and cooking with their kids. And the themes that have emerged from their reflections have included "helping," "lifelong learning," and "sense of belonging."

Sometimes my clients have a number of items that relate to one another, but they struggle to find one word to represent their passion. Ultimately, you want to identify a word or short phrase that feels powerful and acts as an umbrella for several ideas. You might select "connection," for example, which acts as an umbrella for socializing, being with friends, and spending time with family. You might have a passion around "freedom," which might be the umbrella theme covering things like being outdoors in the fresh air, adventure, and homeownership.

As you refine these activities and their underlying passions, remember that they should be really energizing for you. These represent not only how you choose to spend your time but also key aspects of who you are. Once you are able to identify these, not only can you align more of your life activities with these true passions, but you can incorporate them into your purpose statement.

What-I-Love Activities

In his book *The Identity Code*, Larry Ackerman developed an exercise to reveal a person's natural strengths or what he called "innate capacities."[35] I have found this structure equally powerful for uncovering our underlying passions and have adapted it, with his permission:

1 Create five columns in your journal, on a piece of paper, or on your computer.

2 Start by thinking about the activities that you love and make time for. These are your passion projects or what-I-love activities. As you identify them, list your top five across the top of the page, one in each column. Make these activities as specific as you can. For example, if you love reading, is it reading novels, magazines, or nonfiction? If you love to run, is it outdoors or on the treadmill?

3 Underneath your what-I-love activities, make a list of reasons why each matters to you. What makes it important? Why do you enjoy this? What feelings, thoughts, or images does it bring up for you? After each response, ask why one more time. Keep each why to no more than three to four words, and create a list of ten to twelve whys under each activity.

4 Look for connections within and across your columns. Reflect on what your activities have in common. You might consider using colored pens or highlighters to mark the commonalities you see. What themes connect these activities?

5 Think of a word or short phrase to use to represent each of the themes you identify. Summarize these at the bottom

of the page. These reveal your true passions. You can use these alongside your values and strengths as input when creating your purpose statement.

Recognizing Your Strengths

A final dimension that is helpful in exploring our purpose is our *strengths*: character traits, skills, or behaviors that are considered positive. These are ways we excel and differentiate ourselves from others, and they help us to appreciate the impact we have—or want to have—on those around us. Because our strengths are gifts that make us who we are, we can use them to bring our purpose to life.

Remember that your leadership strengths will be evident not only in the workplace but across your life. If you really pinpoint these gifts, you will often notice that you demonstrate them in your personal life as well as your work.

Reflection: Think about the compliments you receive from your family, friends, and colleagues. What strengths are they noticing in you?

Chantal Peyre De Fabregues of BNP Paribas grew up in Africa and was recognized for her strong collaboration and inclusive leadership even as a boarding school student.[36] "My leadership journey really started when I was a child. Even when I was ten or eleven years old, I liked for people to feel included," Peyre De Fabregues said. "I was particularly good at collective sports and found I was often made captain because I spent time ensuring everyone had a role to play." As an adult, Peyre De Fabregues sees these same strengths as essential to her success: "My unique recipe is that I like people. I am always looking for where people are at their best and where they can improve. I enjoy putting together a team in the best possible assemblage to reach our objectives."

While our strengths can take a multitude of forms, success in the twenty-first century is highly dependent on skills relating to social leadership. In addition to looking at our own individual or business success, we need the ability to look more widely at our communities

Strong social leadership requires both a mindset shift around the importance of positive impact and the skills needed to support that shift.

and the environment in which we live and operate. Strong social leadership requires both a mindset shift around the importance of positive impact and the skills needed to support that shift. We will explore the twelve key social leadership skills in depth in chapters 3 through 8, but as a starting point, it's important to understand why these skills matter and how they connect to the societal trends we shared in chapter 1:

- Social leaders form strong connections—We expect more responsiveness and a stronger human relationship with leaders amid digital transformation. In this social era, leaders not only need to hold a real dialogue with their employees and customers, but they also need to rethink their role in society. Employees expect organizations of all forms to act responsibly and with purpose and engage with broader society in a positive way.

- Social leaders establish the context needed for others to succeed—The world has moved from knowledge scarcity to knowledge abundance. It's no longer about what you know but what you can do with what you know. Content expertise is no longer enough. Leaders need to be able to filter through what they hear, see, and read; recognize the patterns; and set the context for others to be successful.

- Social leaders understand the strategic value of social impact—To deliver on their sustainability goals, organizations need social leaders who have the skills, perspectives, and mindset to drive both business results and social impact. Social leaders understand that creating shared value and having a positive societal impact also result in stronger business performance.

Social Leadership Strengths

To explore the concept of social leadership, take the following self-assessment.[37] Read each statement and respond to each on a scale of 1 to 5, where 1 is Completely Disagree and 5 is Completely Agree. Be sure to consider each statement with both work and life outside of work in mind.

After completing the assessment, sum up your score for each skill. Your lowest scores are those you might consider working on further as you proceed through this book. Your highest scores give you clarity on your reason to be and are strengths you can draw on and use in new ways.

CURIOUS

I enjoy learning new things.

I ask a lot of open questions.

I rarely jump to solutions before exploring alternatives.

When I hear about something new, I try to learn more.

I seek out perspectives that are different from my own.

Subtotal

PRESENT

I focus on one thing at a time.

I look people in the eye.

People tell me I'm a good listener.

I am not easily distracted.

I pay attention when someone is speaking to me.

Subtotal

GIVING

I frequently consider the needs of others first.

I often share knowledge and skills with others.

People often acknowledge my contributions.

I make a positive difference.

I am comfortable asking people for help when I need it.

Subtotal

AUTHENTIC

I stay true to what I believe in.

People know the real me.

I am comfortable sharing my true self with other people.

I am honest and open about both my strengths and my weaknesses.

I admit when I make a mistake.

Subtotal

INCLUSIVE

I go out of my way to hear different viewpoints.

I value diverse perspectives.

I proactively surround myself with people who are different from me.

I have a diverse network of colleagues and friends.

I try to work with people who have different working styles from my own.

Subtotal

TRANSPARENT

I am as open as possible with information.

I share information willingly with people who need it.

People describe me as a clear communicator.

I feel comfortable sharing ideas and plans before they are final.

My family and friends know how things are going for me.

Subtotal

FLEXIBLE

I am open to new input when making a decision.

I appreciate hearing other points of view.

I am willing to change my mind.

I enthusiastically learn new things and apply the learning to my work.

I am willing to compromise.

Subtotal

RESOURCEFUL

I am good at seeing patterns and connections.

I know where to go to find solutions.

I enjoy experimenting and innovating.

People describe me as creative.

I know when to trust my own judgment.

Subtotal

COURAGEOUS

I take appropriate risks.

I make decisions that are unpopular if I feel they are right.

I speak up and share my views, even when it's difficult.

I question why things are the way they are.

When faced with a new challenge, I have confidence to try a different approach.

Subtotal

INSPIRING

I motivate other people to take action.

I bring things to life for people.

I lead by example.

I inspire others to be passionate about what I love.

I am good at convincing other people to take part in something.

Subtotal

ACCOUNTABLE

If I promise something, I can be relied upon to do it.

I am comfortable sharing responsibility with others.

I accept the consequences of my actions.

People know they can trust me to deliver what I say I will.

I have high expectations of myself and of other people.

Subtotal

COLLABORATIVE

I proactively reach out to others to get their input.

I enjoy working with other people.

I feel comfortable sharing decisions with others.

People describe me as a good team player.

I incorporate other people's input.

Subtotal

Your Purpose Statement

Once you have identified your values, passions, and strengths, you can craft a *purpose statement* that encapsulates your reason to be. A purpose can and should be aspirational. None of us lives in alignment with our purpose all the time, but being able to express it with conviction and clarity allows us to make decisions about where we focus, helps inspire us to make better choices, and provides greater self-awareness, which leads to more satisfaction.

In their book *Find Your Why*, David Mead, Peter Docker, and Simon Sinek provided a simple structure for what they call a Why Statement.[38] This includes two parts: the actions you will take and the contribution you will make. I recommend you use this similar format when writing your purpose statement. It can be expressed in this form:

My purpose is to (take this action)
so that (I have this impact).

Here are some examples of inspiring purpose statements developed by people I've encountered at workshops and whose well-chosen words I would like to share:

- "My purpose is to improve the self-worth of people around the world so that they can contribute fully to society."

- "My purpose is to help level the playing field so everyone has an equal opportunity to succeed."

- "My purpose is to enable people to be their best selves so that they can lead fulfilled and happy lives."

- "My purpose is to encourage innovative and forward-thinking ideas to improve the lives of others."

Being able to express our purpose with conviction and clarity allows us to make decisions about where we focus, helps inspire us to make better choices, and provides greater self-awareness.

Crafting Your Purpose Statement

To help you craft this powerful sentence for yourself, reflect back on the words and concepts that emerged from your work on values, passions, and strengths:

1 *Capture the specific words you identified*—It can be helpful to note them down on a Venn diagram, like the following one, to see how they overlap and what meanings arise. Include not only your passions (the themes that connect your interests) but the top five what-I-love activities as well.

2 *Create a first draft of your purpose statement*—I recommend using this structure: "My purpose is to (take this action) so that (I have this impact)."

3 *Reflect on your draft statement's relevance in many domains of your life*—Bear in mind that your purpose statement is most powerful if it covers who you are across both the personal and professional. In working with my clients, I notice that many people struggle to bring their work and home lives together under one purpose. It's quite common that a purpose statement focuses on work activities and the commitment we are making to our organizations while leaving behind who we are in other parts of our lives. I challenge you to try to bring these parts together and consider them as one whole: If you are working today, what would your purpose be if you retired tomorrow? If your purpose is clear outside your work, how can you bring it to life in the workplace? Where do you see your values, strengths, and passions in each of these domains? The more you can provide equal weight to these as you craft your purpose statement, the more impactful it will be for you.

4 *Share your draft statement with a close friend or colleague*—Listen to how they respond to this and the questions they ask. Revise if needed or desired.

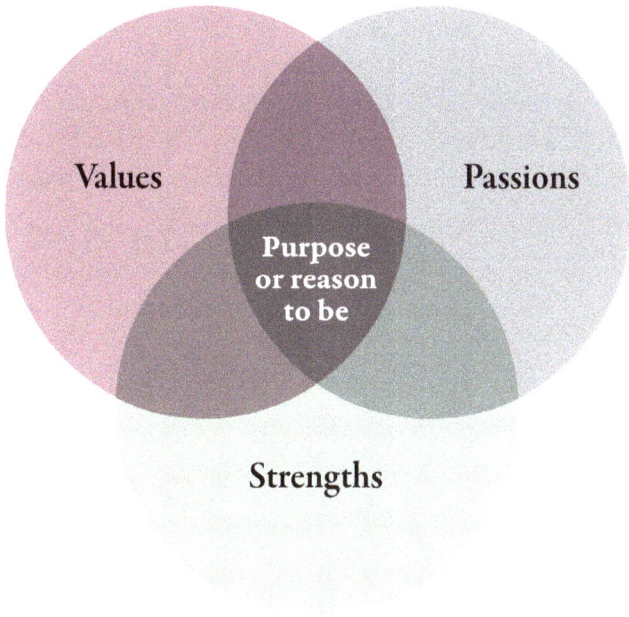

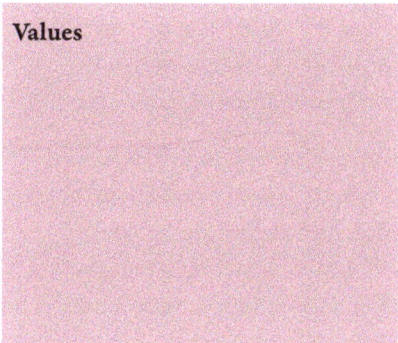

Values

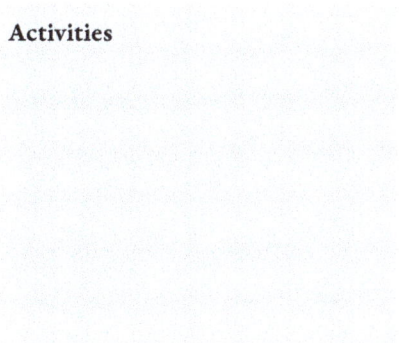

Activities

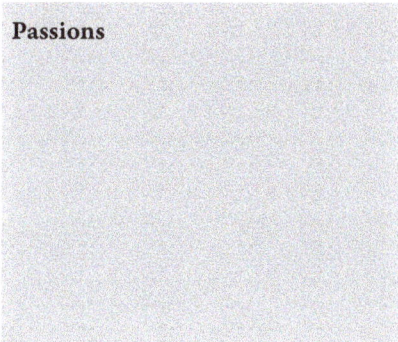

Passions

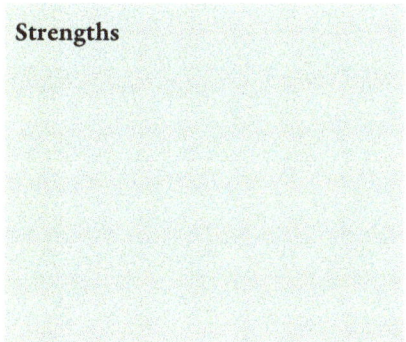

Strengths

Take Action

Here are some ways you can strengthen and apply the work we have done in this chapter. You can think of these as *micro assignments*. Don't try to take on too much all at once. You might consider selecting one that feels most relevant for you, then move on when you're ready.

1 *Make your purpose visible*—Type or write your purpose on a poster or small flyer that you can hang near your work-space or on your refrigerator. I typed mine in large font, added some photos representing my strengths, passions, activities, and values, and printed it out. I laminated it and hung it next to my desk in my office. You can be as creative as you like; the important thing is that you hang it up in a place where you can see it and revisit it regularly.

2 *Share with a colleague, client, or new acquaintance*—The next time someone asks you to share something about your-self, be courageous and share your purpose as part of this description. This can make you feel vulnerable the first time you do it, but it gets easier with practice. Sharing this can help you to validate that you have captured some-thing real and help you refine your thinking.

3 *Consider the how*—Take some time to define how you bring this statement to life across your personal and pro-fessional lives today. What do you do at work that is reinforcing this purpose? What about in your personal life? In your personal life, you might consider how you interact with your family members, your friends, your community, or any clubs or groups you belong to. Would they recognize this purpose in the way you behave and the ways you choose to spend your time?

4 *Keep your purpose alive*—Set up a reminder to look at your purpose statement on a monthly basis. Check in with yourself in regard to how you are prioritizing and how aligned your life and decisions are to this vision.

Your purpose is foundational to being an impactful social leader. With this clear and inspiring statement in hand, we will head into the next chapter to learn about how authenticity strengthens relationships and supports your quest toward positive leadership.

Leading with Courageous Authenticity

Because the courage to be authentic is the foundation for deeper relationships

REFLECTION

Think of a person you have worked with who was authentic or inauthentic. What made you feel that way about them?

"Abandon the idea of being fearless. Instead, walk directly into your fears, with your values as your guide, towards what matters to you. Courage is not the absence of fear; courage is fear walking."

—Susan David, psychologist

S atya Nadella was only eight months into his role as CEO of Microsoft in 2014 when he was invited onstage for a conversation with Maria Klawe at the Grace Hopper Celebration of Women in Computing. Klawe, a computer scientist, president of Harvey Mudd College, and member of Microsoft's board of directors, asked Nadella what women should do if they felt uncomfortable asking for a raise. His guidance, which perhaps not surprisingly faced broad criticism, was that women shouldn't ask for raises but should trust "karma" and believe that the system would eventually reward their work.

I was an employee at Microsoft at the time, and I remember the email he sent before he left for the conference, expressing excitement over the opportunity to attend and learn, and then the one he sent afterward and also published online, publicly apologizing for his comments.

What is striking about this situation, even years later, is that what could have been a devastating misstep in the early days of a very visible CEO was tempered by the authenticity with which he issued his apology and responded to the resulting backlash. While the immediate response was explosive, the story became one balanced with praise for his vulnerability, honesty, and humility, and some said the lessons Nadella learned from the experience left him more prepared to lead the company into the future.

As an employee—and a female one at that—who might have been offended by Nadella's original comments, I believed that he learned from his mistake and gave him credit for talking so quickly and transparently about what happened. I don't expect perfection from executives, but I do expect to see them acknowledge it when they don't get things right. For me, this was a real example of courageous authenticity.

What Is Authenticity?

Being an *authentic leader* means we share our "true selves" with those around us. On a practical level, this looks like being honest and open about strengths and weaknesses, admitting mistakes, and expressing a certain degree of vulnerability.

> *We regard leaders as authentic when their conduct is in congruence with what they truly believe.*

We regard leaders as authentic when their conduct is in congruence with what they truly believe. Without authenticity, we are unable to establish real connections. It is true connection, as well as the sense of belonging it creates, that is essential for our well-being. As Brené Brown described in *The Atlas of the Heart*, "We have to belong to ourselves as much as we belong to others. Any belonging that asks us to betray ourselves is not true belonging."[39]

When I ask my clients what it means to be authentic, I hear words you'd expect like *real, honest, transparent, removing barriers, sincere, genuine, being yourself*—and I hear *courageous*. I would agree with this. True authenticity requires us to expose ourselves, our views, and our mistakes, and that requires courage.

In the book *Authentic*, Professor Stephen Joseph used this formula for authentic living:

Know yourself + Own yourself + Be yourself = the Authentic Life[40]

According to Joseph, authentic people first know who they are and what motivates them; second, they own their decisions, their mistakes, and their faults; and finally, they have the courage to behave in alignment with their beliefs. If any one of these components is missing, it's no longer true authenticity.

All of this starts with courage.

The Courage to Be Real

Understanding your core values is essential for authenticity. Without an understanding of our values and an ability to articulate them, we struggle to share our genuine selves with others. Authenticity is about being true to yourself and behaving in alignment with your values in your daily life and decisions.

Generally, when we allow ourselves to be authentic at work and make decisions aligned with our values, we also permit ourselves to express a wider range of emotions. This has positive consequences for us as individuals, leading to greater well-being and higher performance. It also allows people around us to connect to us in richer ways.

Bayile Adeoti is the founder of Dechomai, a Scottish social enterprise focused on empowering ethnic minority communities with enterprise skills.[41] She said that she found that her work with women during the pandemic helped her learn to be more authentic. "I used to keep myself to myself and never showed all of me," Adeoti said. "But I realized when you share about yourself and about your journey, this is what people relate to."

Adeoti extended this vulnerability to being open around her mistakes and failures. She hopes this inspires others. "I love to talk about my failures, but also how I got up from every single one," she said. "Maybe it helps people stay on track and say, 'Oh, you know what; I remember when Bayile had a bad day. This is just like Bayile's bad day. I can keep going.'"

Adeoti also expressed that the pandemic led her to be more authentic in her leadership style, and though this may sound counterintuitive, she is not the only one who felt that way. At the start of the pandemic, when many countries went into lockdown and organizations were forced to make dramatic shifts in their ways of working, there was a surge of online socialization. In an attempt to reduce isolation and offer support in this strange new world we were all navigating, many companies organized Zoom coffees and online games. Even the most unlikely industries created recipe swaps, haiku competitions, and team scavenger hunts.

But as the pandemic continued, this investment started taking a back seat, and many of my clients felt they didn't have time to socialize. They started questioning the value of online team building, and I heard comments like "We are going to wait for that team building until we can go for drinks after work again" or "We can't really do team building because we can't meet in person."

In fact, research has suggested that the time spent on building relationships and finding shared interests—even when these

Authenticity is about being true to yourself and behaving in alignment with your values in your daily life and decisions.

opportunities are possible only virtually—correlates with positive business impact. A study by Ron Friedman in *Harvard Business Review* found that high-performing team members were 25 percent more likely to spend time at the office discussing nonwork matters with their colleagues than those on average teams.[42]

While it's not uncommon to feel that this time spent on relationship building is a distraction from the business, these social activities (and the skills required to support them) are equally important to those focused on getting tasks done. What may seem initially like an either-or decision—*Should I focus on relationships, or should I focus on tasks?*—is actually what's called a *polarity*, a both-and situation containing seemingly opposing ideas. We don't have to choose between building connections and getting the job done. They are intertwined and equally essential.

> *Reflection: What does it feel like when you are being real with your colleagues or employees? How does that compare with how you feel being real with your family and friends?*

The authenticity supported through this relationship building also leads to higher-performing teams. Friedman found that members of high-performing teams were significantly more likely to express positive emotions with their teammates, including compliments and jokes. They were more likely to use emojis, GIFs, and exclamation points in emails. But what might be surprising is that the higher-performing teams also were more likely to express negative emotions through sarcasm, complaints, and even cursing. Friedman attributed this to the cognitive cost of suppressing emotion. When we don't share our authentic selves, we expend brain resources hiding our true thoughts, feelings, and values from others, and this leaves less mental energy for productive work. When we feel we are able to express our full range of emotions, it frees us up and leads to better performance.

Brené Brown would agree, adding that vulnerability is the most necessary ingredient for authentic connection. In her book *Daring Greatly* and her viral 2010 TED talk, Brown argued that while vulnerability is often perceived as a weakness, it actually requires profound courage.[43] Her work centers on research that shows that vulnerability is a strength and can lead to enhanced creativity, stronger connections, and greater joy.

EXERCISE

Share Something Real

Find a situation where you can share something real with your colleagues and choose in that moment to be vulnerable. This lets others see that you are human, just like them, helping you create connections that are richer and more meaningful. You can encourage others to share by asking open, curious questions that allow for more meaningful conversations. Surprising questions that can lead to rich learnings include the following:

- What was your first leadership role?

- How do you like to learn?

- You've probably had several career highlights; which one are you most proud of?

- What's the worst job you ever had, and what did you learn from it?

- What career advice would you give your younger self?

- What is your favorite way to spend a day off?

- What activity instantly calms you?

At Be Leadership, we practice sharing something real through what we call "Spotlight." At the start of each of our team meetings, one member of the team is selected to be "in the spotlight." That person selects two questions from a list like this one and shares the answers with the rest of us. This allows each person to choose what to share and how vulnerable to be, while helping us to get to know each other better.

The Courage to Be Imperfect

Early in my career, I worked with a business leader who was incredibly competent. In several years of working with her, I never saw her arrive unprepared. She was polished, poised, and professional. Another leader described her as "buttoned up" and confided that he had never seen her appear flustered in what were countless stressful conversations.

Reading this, you probably are imagining a highly capable business leader, and she was. She didn't share anything before it was fully formed, and she placed a high value on ensuring her faults were hidden from view. But with all this polish, it was hard to get beneath the surface. Not only could we not see her imperfections, but we also didn't really know much about who she was and what she stood for. As a result, she demonstrated competence but didn't inspire followership. Her team around her commented that they didn't know her and that their connection with her felt shallow.

This leader stayed at the organization for years. She was admired for her professional skills, but she did not form strong connections with her team or other stakeholders. And ultimately, she left the business without progressing to a new role. What she wasn't conveying with all this professionalism was authenticity.

In contrast with this, Microsoft's Jean-Philippe Courtois has learned the value of vulnerability. When I asked him about times he was at his best as a leader, he shared a story of true courageous authenticity. Courtois, whose Microsoft career spans nearly forty years and who is currently serving as executive vice president and president of National Transformation Partnerships at Microsoft, described a time when, as a senior executive, he agreed to be coached in front of three thousand members of his management team.

At the time, Courtois was leading the Microsoft global sales organization, and he needed to help his team transform from selling software licenses to becoming trusted advisors for customers undertaking digital transformation. Because he saw the importance of developing coaching skills as part of this change, he was going through coaching himself and decided to undertake a public coaching session. Going onstage alongside Michael Bungay Stanier, author of the book *The Coaching Habit*, Courtois was coached around his own leadership challenges. "It was embarrassing because for sure people could see me struggling with some of his questions and could see some big doubts I had about transforming the sales organization," Courtois said.[44]

But the vulnerability paid off. "I received so many notes from people in that room telling me, 'JP, that was the most exciting moment I've seen of you.'" As a result, Courtois saw increased commitment around the transformation, his leadership, and coaching as a skillset: "Doing what you ask your people to do was something that was really appreciated by people. It created a deep, intimate connection with me they had not seen before."

Leaders who come across as infallible risk cultivating an environment in which their employees and teams feel unable to express concern, dissent, or uncertainty. This can lead to large, damaging errors. In contrast, leaders like Nadella and Courtois who admit their faults and share their own misgivings create a vulnerability loop in which other members of the team also feel able to share. This helps to build trust.

Encouraging leaders to be courageous around mistakes and failures has business benefits too. Some organizations see their rapid risk-taking and learning from failure as giving them a competitive edge. Mark Zuckerberg told early Facebook employees to "move fast and break things," which became an internal motto used by the company until 2014.[45] While this attitude received some criticism for under-emphasizing quality, a positive mindset around accepting—or even rewarding—failure is a core principle of many technology companies.

According to Pixar's cofounder Ed Catmull, the animation studio has adopted this cultural mindset too: "By proactively removing the negative connotations around failure, the project team can push the boundaries of risk and break new creative ground in their films," Catmull said. "The worst mistake an employee or leader can make is to base decisions solely on avoiding error."[46]

I heard a similar sentiment from Bryan Nixon, the head of TASIS England, an international school in Surrey. "I'm not so worried that people make mistakes," he said. "In fact, if they don't make mistakes, I wonder if we've actually changed or challenged anything. What I'm more interested in is hearing what they learned. I don't need people to beat themselves up. I want them to tell me how we either avoid this or think about it in a completely different way so that we grow from it."[47]

The Courage to Know When to Speak

You probably know the name Malala Yousafzai. A Pakistani activist and 2014 Nobel Peace Prize laureate, she is known for fighting for justice and equality for girls and women all around the world. She is an inspiration due to her courage in facing adversity and famously said, "When the whole world is silent, even one voice becomes powerful."[48]

It is true that courage is often about speaking up in a space where no one else wants to share their views, but so is the opposite. Former prime minister of the United Kingdom Winston Churchill is apocryphally credited to have said, "Courage is what it takes to stand up and speak, and courage is also what it takes to sit down and listen."[49] Whether fact or legend, this sentiment is also true.

Now, you might be thinking, *I'm not Malala or Churchill. I can't be courageous like that.* So let me be clear that courage takes many forms. In the book *Choosing Courage*, Jim Detert made a strong point that we all have opportunities to be what he called "competently courageous" in the decisions we make each day.[50] When we think we have to be the Malalas and Churchills of the world to act with courage, it isn't helpful. We are putting them on a pedestal and think we can't achieve that because we're not superhuman. Detert reminds us that they are no more superhuman than us. They have made brave choices in their lives. Being courageous is about making brave choices every minute of every day.

I heard this powerful story from Deise Nogueira, a leader in one of Be Leadership's workshops:

> I remember two things that happened to me—one a very long time ago and one not so long ago. And I truly believe the first situation shaped how I behave as a leader now.
>
> When I was in my early twenties, I was in my first leadership role, and my boss told me how to manage my team. At that time, I didn't agree with him, but I didn't speak up. It's very clear to me now that the people that I was responsible

for back then felt lost. So I learned what happens when I don't behave with courage.

More recently, the same thing happened. But, thank God, I remembered how I felt after the first situation, and I could behave differently the second time. I stayed with my values and handled things differently. I could see the difference in the trust on the team and how well people responded when they felt they could trust me as their leader. So, for me, the most important [lesson] was [that] much trust is lost in leadership when people see that we are not behaving, and leading, in a courageous way.

These decisions around whether to speak up are not always black and white. Sometimes we face situations where it's unclear where the courageous decision lies: Is it speaking up when you encounter someone who has a different viewpoint from you? Or is it more courageous to stay silent and listen to the other perspective? Sometimes silence is the better answer, but we jump in too quickly. And sometimes we don't speak up when we should.

Reflection: Think of a recent situation where you had to decide whether to speak up. How courageous were you in the moment? How would you hope to respond next time if faced with something similar?

While we won't always make the right choice in the moment, we can use these scenarios as opportunities for reflection and growth.

Take Action

Both courage and authenticity are defined by the choices you make every minute of every day. Review the following actions and select something you are motivated to change. Work on it until it feels complete or habitual, and then move on to something else. Small changes make a big difference.

1 *Reflect on your level of courage*—At the end of each day, ask yourself whether you have been courageous in your decision-making. Courageous leaders choose to do what's difficult, and to keep doing that every day. Remember that courage is a virtue developed with practice, a muscle that must be strengthened day by day and choice by choice. Ask yourself, *What is the impact when I lead with courageous authenticity on myself? On my teams? On the organization?*

2 *Ask, "I don't know. What do you think?"*—Start asking, "I don't know. What do you think?" This is an admission that you don't have all the answers and need help, and it allows someone else to share their views. As a leader, you are often paid to have answers and resolve issues for people. But you *can't* have all the answers in a world changing at this pace. Admitting you don't know, need help, and want input allows for better outcomes while developing a stronger team culture.

3 *Listen to feedback*—Proactively ask for feedback on your leadership, and listen carefully to what is shared. Feedback can be difficult to hear, but seeking it out and, importantly, accepting it is one of the most courageous things you can do to accelerate your development and enhance your leadership. Try asking open questions such as these:

- *"What am I doing as a leader that is helpful for you?"*
- *"What could I do that would make me even more effective?"*
- *"How do you feel about being part of this team?"*
- *"What would you like us to do more or less of?"*

4 *Encourage healthy debate*—Promote constructive disagreement and healthy debate. When you allow employees to give feedback not only on your ideas but also on the ideas and tasks that the entire team is working on, it fosters invention, creativity, and risk-taking.

5 *Celebrate mistakes*—Discuss mistakes and situations that haven't gone according to plan. This helps to create a culture where mistakes aren't disasters; rather, they are learning opportunities. It is through failure that we learn and grow and innovate. Instead of dwelling on the mistake, talk about what you learned from it and how you can do things differently next time. Build a team where the team members know that if something goes wrong, you'll be in their corner.

6 *Choose authentic action*—Find something that you feel a bit scared of representing and choose to take a stand. As part of this, listen respectfully to the opposition, and decide what courageous step to take. Sometimes this is speaking up, and sometimes this is staying silent. "Authentic interaction can be choosing to conform to demands or pushing back," Karissa Thacker wrote in *The Art of Authenticity*. "Authentic action takes into account both you and the situation."[51] Choosing authentic action can be particularly courageous when those around you aren't acting with authenticity. Work culture is influenced by every team member, so small changes, made with courage, can have wider impact.

I want you to really go out there and practice courageous authenticity. Remember: what you role model, you get back. It's amazing how the authentic culture you create as a leader gets mirrored back at you. Also keep in mind that it's not about perfection; it's about practice, which leads us to what we'll discuss in the next chapter: cultivating curiosity and openness so you can utilize a beginner's mindset.

Adopting a Beginner's Mindset

Because by keeping an open mind, you can move beyond your limiting beliefs

REFLECTION

When was the last time you tried something for the first time?

"The ability to learn is the most important quality a leader can have."

—Padmasree Warrior, technology executive

When you think of Albert Einstein, what comes to mind? Nearly every time I ask this of our clients, the first word that comes up is either *intelligent* or *genius*.

Einstein probably deserves these labels. He was an incredible physicist and Nobel Prize winner who helped to shape our understanding of the universe, and he changed the world with his theories and discoveries. But personally, he didn't attribute his success to intelligence. Instead, he said, "I have no special talents. I am only passionately curious."[52]

There are many urban legends about Einstein's life, and it's hard to separate fact from fiction. However, it's rarely disputed that Einstein was passionate about lifelong learning and he loved to ask questions.

Here are some questions I have for you:

- What does it mean to step back from a position of knowing and assume you don't have the answers?
- How do you wipe the slate clean in your thinking and remove the biases, assumptions, and knowledge that you have accumulated?

By the time we reach adulthood, operating without our ingrained biases is nearly impossible. Our brains, which are exceptional at seeing patterns and making connections, compare every new experience and question to something that has come before. While this helps us learn more quickly, it also hinders our ability to see things from a fresh point of view. In this chapter, we are going to channel Einstein's openness around curiosity and learning and think about what it takes to develop a beginner's mindset.

How to Get Curious

What does curiosity look like in practice? When asked this in Be Leadership workshops, participants talk about open-mindedness, asking questions, modesty, and encouraging others' opinions.

Einstein has advice on this too: "If I had an hour to solve a problem and my life depended on the solution, I would spend the first fifty-five minutes determining the proper question to ask, for once I

> *Curious leaders are always learning. They understand, accept, and admit when they don't know something.*

know the proper question, I could solve the problem in less than five minutes."[53] The point being made here is that stepping back and being curious about the problem you're trying to solve needs to come before solutioning.

Curious leaders are always learning. They understand, accept, and admit when they don't know something. These leaders explore ideas with an open mind, look for novel solutions to old problems, seek out additional perspectives, and identify new ways to think and behave.

Questions are at the heart of curiosity. They add value because they offer us the opportunity to do the following:

- Be creative and uncover new breakthrough ideas and solutions by drawing on the insights of others.
- Build relationships and demonstrate engagement. People respond more positively to questions than if they are just told things.
- Step back and get perspective to reflect on what we know and don't know.
- Explore new avenues before coming to a decision.

When we're problem-solving, there is value in first diverging, through open, curious questions, before we converge toward solutions. This helps us broaden and expand our thinking. For this we need to use open questions or questions that do not require a yes or no answer. Open questions typically start with *how*, *what*, or *why* and prompt the respondent to give a descriptive answer. We use open questions when we want to gather as much information as possible or get perspectives we are not even expecting. Open questions encourage innovation and creativity.

In contrast, closed questions, answerable by either yes or no, help us get to the point and clarify a situation. They are valuable when trying to drive consensus, move us forward, and close down discussion or decisions.

While closed questions can also bring value, the opportunity here is to expand your use of open questions. As humans, we often use closed questions when we intend to use open ones. We may be implying an open question but asking it in a closed way. This makes the question less powerful. Here are a few examples of common closed questions and more powerful open alternatives:

Closed Questions	Open Question Alternatives
Does this shirt look good on me?	What do you think of this outfit?
Did you have a good day?	What happened at school today?
Do you have exciting plans for the weekend?	What do you have going on this weekend?
Are you needing help with that?	How can I help?
Are you going to get that project done on time?	How is it going with the project?

Because closed questions are so prevalent, as listeners we are trained to interpret them as open and extend our answers. But the way in which the question is asked closes down our thinking and creates bias.

An intentionally crafted open question is far more powerful. Joël Stofer, a participant in a recent workshop, made this observation: "Open questions automatically trigger new questions. It's like you have a door in front of you, and you open it. Then in the next room, you have three doors."

Reflection: How conscious are you of the kinds of questions you ask? How often are your questions unintentionally closed?

Child's Mind, Beginner's Mind

When my daughter was young, she, like all other children, first learned about the world through experimentation, trial and error, imitation, and play. She used to enjoy opening my wallet and taking out every membership card, photo, credit card, and receipt. She dumped my change onto the table and sorted the coins by size. As adults, we know what these objects look and feel like; we don't need to pull them all out and hold them. But a child learns through this exploration.

In addition to this discovery process, children ask challenging, open questions to try to make sense of what they see and experience. Once when my daughter was two or three, we were driving through London, and she spotted a man sleeping in a doorway. She asked, "Why is that man sleeping there?" The simple answer—"because he is homeless"—only leads to more questions. Children are excellent at asking profound questions, and part of the reason for this is their instinct for curiosity.

I was fortunate to study with Michael Marquardt, a George Washington University professor and cofounder of the World Institute for Action Learning. He described this childhood learning process as a time of incredible discovery and growth. Unlike adults, who are constrained by social norms, children are uninhibited in their exploration. So, as Marquardt described, they don't mind rummaging through someone else's handbag or asking embarrassing questions. And through this process of discovery, they experience a steep learning curve. Yet when society discourages the exploration and the questions, that curve flattens.[54]

Children inherently operate with a *beginner's mind*, a Buddhist concept described by Zen monk Shunryū Suzuki in his book *Zen Mind, Beginner's Mind*. He wrote, "In the beginner's mind, there are many possibilities, but in the expert's there are few."[55] Having a beginner's mindset, then, means approaching every situation with open, child-like wonder instead of intellectual overconfidence. This makes us adaptable, responsive to change, and open to new ideas. As adults, most of us struggle to maintain this level of flexibility. Some people, however, stand out as practitioners of lifelong learning.

My colleague, organizational development consultant Anita

Bhasin, approaches the world in this way. Through changing professions and moving around the world, she has always been proactive in seeking out learning along the way. She said, "I'm very fond of the term *versatilist*, which was introduced to me by one of my professors, Chris Worley [at Pepperdine University]. If you're not a generalist or a specialist, but you're a versatilist, you can morph and adapt to what's needed in the moment. I have used this as a way of staying agile."[56]

Bhasin said she maintains this attitude with a mantra of sorts—"plan tight so you can hang loose." This helped me understand the beginner's mind as a combination of curiosity and flexibility. This doesn't mean being unprepared, but it does mean fostering a willingness to see beyond the box and adjust your plans.

Reflection: How can you be a versatilist, both in your personal and professional life?

Particularly now, when it's unlikely we'll stay in one career throughout our lifetime, it's useful to retain an open-minded attitude like Bhasin's. This relies on two sets of skills that we can practice and develop: The first relates to expansive curiosity and the generation of questions. And the second is following questions through to actual experience without making assumptions. Retaining a beginner's mindset into our adulthood helps us diverge, expand, remain creative, and avoid dead ends. This allows us to solve problems we face each day even if they are novel and difficult.

Retaining a beginner's mindset into our adulthood helps us diverge, expand, remain creative, and avoid dead ends.

Flexible Leadership

There is no shortage of complex and ambiguous problems in today's world. We have societal challenges relating to climate change, economic crisis, and political conflict. We have rapidly evolving diseases that don't care about international borders. With advances in technology, we face new questions around data privacy and the ethics of AI. Our working and living environments are constantly undergoing change, sometimes at an accelerating rate. In chapter 1, I shared the fact that new types of jobs and roles that don't exist right now are expected to increase dramatically in the next decade. We all must have a beginner's mindset to stay ahead of these changes.

Whatever situations we face, we benefit from staying flexible. Leaders who can draw on this skill are more likely to overcome hurdles. One such leader is Peter Muthaura, director of training and strategic partnerships for Human Needs Project, an organization in Kenya that helps people break out of poverty by providing them with essential infrastructure. "I approach challenges with an awareness that what I think are the solutions may not be," Muthaura said.[57] "There could be other, better ideas or the circumstances could change, calling for a different approach."

Muthaura said when he approaches his work with this level of adaptability, it reduces his stress levels and also benefits other people around him. He gave this example:

> Just the other day, I was running a Sprint program for digital microwork, and I had a very strict target around the number of people I should train, which was set by the funding partner. After screening people, sharing expectations, and conducting an orientation, I realized that some people were still dropping out. I was getting a little bit nervous and wondered how I should handle this. I wanted to have 120 people complete the Sprint. I already had lost eight. What was going to happen?

Muthaura didn't have enough time to run a makeup class for those who missed the early lessons, yet every session was required and needed to be attended in a specific order. He needed a new, creative solution. A junior colleague came up with the idea of getting back in touch with people who had shown interest but hadn't made it through the screening process and bringing on an extra trainer to get them up to speed.

In this situation, everyone benefited: Not only did Muthaura and Human Needs Project meet their target, but more people had a learning opportunity. Muthaura added that the flexibility also ensured his colleague's input was incorporated: "Nothing is more inspiring than knowing that your views and suggestions are really valued."

As leaders, we are paid to solve problems, and we're rewarded for solutions. And that causes us to internalize what coach and author Jennifer Garvey Berger called a *mindtrap*, something that stops us from being curious and pulls us away from a beginner's mindset.[58] So what is this thing that's limiting us? Our assumption that we are right.

How Are You Listening?

Consider the following scenarios and reflect on how you are most likely to respond.

- *Scenario 1: You're presenting something to colleagues for approval. You've been working on it for weeks, and you are just trying to get final sign-off. Most of the team members listen to the presentation and offer support. But one person starts to ask questions that no one has raised before in all the weeks that you've been working on it.*

  What is your reaction? Do you get defensive? Are you concerned that you've missed something important? Are you frustrated that they are bringing this up now? Or are you open and curious about the new input and flexible enough to consider it?

- *Scenario 2: An employee comes to you, their manager, with an urgent question about their work. You haven't been directly involved with this project, but it's within your broad remit and an area in which you have a lot of expertise. The deadline is looming.*

  What's your reaction here? Are you impatient and concerned? Do you think, *I should have done this myself?* Do you tell the employee what to do because of the deadline? Or are you open and curious? Do you ask questions like "What have you tried so far?" or "What do you think?"

These are both scenarios where you might get trapped by rightness.

If you highly value curiosity, or this is one of your strengths, you are more likely to respond in an open way, but many people find these types of situations difficult. One way to avoid this "right-ness" mindtrap is to reflect on the way in which you are listening. Consider this question: What situations cause you to slip into assuming you know best?

Three Ways to Listen

In her book *Unlocking Leadership Mindtraps: How to Thrive in Complexity*, Berger described three different ways that you can listen in any situation:[59]

1 *Listening to win*—This is basically telling the other person they're wrong, even if it's for generous reasons and you're nice about it. The message you give back when you listen to win is one of negation or dismissal—"I'm sure it's not as bad as you think" or "Thanks, but we've already tried that."

2 *Listening to fix*—When we listen in this way, we are searching for a solution or an answer. All of us in leadership roles can fall prey to this because we're often rewarded early on in our careers when we do this. Responses when we are listening to fix often take the form of "What if we try this?" or "Have you thought about this?" Even if it's framed as a question, it's driving toward a specific outcome.

3 *Listening to learn*—This is the type of listening where we try to understand the other person's perspective *as they understand it*. It's important to remember that there's subjective truth. Sometimes more than one person is right. What's helpful is to be curious about why we feel the way that we do and to try to really understand the other person's perspective. We hold off from jumping to a solution or an answer, and we try to understand.

What's similar about the first two forms of listening is that they start from an assumption that we know more than the person we are speaking to—that we are right, and they need to come around to our point of view.

When we listen to learn, we are practicing both curiosity and flexibility. We're being open to different perspectives. Our curiosity allows us to take in and incorporate these ideas into our view of the world. This allows us to learn not only if we're successful but also if we fail. We learn not only if we're right but also if we're wrong. Now that's powerful stuff.

When we listen to learn, we are practicing both curiosity and flexibility.

Reset Your Mindset

In recent years, a lot has been shared around the work of Carol Dweck, who describes two mindsets: fixed mindset and growth mindset.[60] Dweck's work is used widely to help aid development and to shift the way that you think about the sort of challenges that you face.

If you have a fixed mindset, you are focused on your intelligence and current abilities. You're very aware of your own skills and know where your gaps are. But you also assume that that's the way it will always be, so you are fixed in the way you see your talent and how you can apply it. With a fixed mindset, you are likely to use phrases that start with "I'm not very good at . . ." These might be comments like "I'm not very good at math," "I'm not detail oriented," "I'm not very good at public speaking," or "I can't learn that new technology." Operating with a fixed mindset means you assume the situation is predetermined and unchangeable. Even further, you assume *you* can't change. You instead find other ways to cope, such as asking someone else to do the work for you, because they can do it "better."

A growth mindset is just the opposite. A growth mindset is the idea that when you are in a particular situation, the limits are nonexistent or shiftable. You see your current limitations as opportunities to learn, and you are flexible in terms of your view of yourself and your ability. You see the "future you" as being very different from the "current you." With a growth mindset, you see mistakes as opportunities to improve, and you are less daunted by setbacks.

At TASIS England school, Bryan Nixon encourages a growth

mindset: "I'm very comfortable with saying what we can do and what we can't do. I'm also very confident in saying what we've achieved, but also what we haven't. And I see that as part of a journey. This is what it means to have a growth mindset."[61]

Jean-Philippe Courtois similarly described how focusing on a growth mindset and being more curious has helped him enhance his leadership at Microsoft: "Over the last many years as we have transformed into a cloud- and AI-first company, I have had to become a lot more curious in order to achieve more. This means speaking less and listening a lot more in all kinds of interactions with people—with my team members, one-to-one relationships, one-to-few, with customers, one to many."[62] Courtois also noted that when he is completely present with people and approaches conversations with a curious mindset, it allows him to fully listen and understand people's challenges.

It's worth remembering that mindset can be context dependent. You may generally be very growth minded but remain fixed in specific domains. My colleague Richard Strudwick, a leadership development consultant and coach, appreciates his ability to learn and grow and is open and flexible around learning new skills. Yet when rock climbing, a sport his wife loves, Strudwick doesn't think he's any good.[63]

One straightforward way to think about the difference between fixed and growth mindsets—and to shift to be more open to growth in domains where you are a bit stuck—is to consider your use of the word *yet*. "I'm not good at math" is a fixed-mindset statement. It assumes little ability to change. But adding the word *yet*—"I'm not good at math yet"—expresses a willingness to consider the possibility for improvement.

EXERCISE

Where Is Your Mindset?

To start expanding your mindset, it's useful to consider the ways in which your views are fixed. To help you reflect on this, read the following pairs of statements, adapted from Dweck's work. For each statement, consider whether your attitude is closer to the left or right side. It might be helpful to brainstorm some recent situations where these thoughts might have popped up. Keep in mind that your answers might be different depending on the context.

Fixed Mindset		Growth Mindset
Intelligence and talent are static.	←→	Intelligence and talent can be developed.
I see constructive feedback as criticism.	←→	I see constructive feedback as an opportunity to learn.
Stretching beyond what I know is risky and always includes a degree of failure.	←→	Stretching myself into uncomfortable spaces is helpful for development and improves my abilities.
I am motivated by being accomplished and good at things.	←→	I am motivated by getting better and improving.
I like to focus on things I'm good at.	←→	I like to try new things.
I see the success of others as an indication I'm not working hard enough.	←→	I see the success of others as a learning opportunity.

The statements on the left represent views that are more fixed or closed. It is likely that if you've selected statements on the left-hand side, they are restricting your potential, and therefore represent an opportunity for you to develop as a curious and flexible leader.

If you look through these and think about your life, which represents the greatest opportunity for you? Which might be a self-limiting belief that if shifted would give you an opportunity to grow and move forward?

Take Action

As we've explored throughout this chapter, curiosity and flexibility are skills that help you develop a mindset that is more open to learning, sparking new ideas and insights, and leading to breakthroughs and success. Here are a few suggestions for ways you can practice being flexible and curious.

1. *WAIT (Why am I talking?)*—The next time you feel you want to jump in and share something, pause and consider this acronym: WAIT. *Why am I talking?* Sometimes our need to describe our own experience or share our opinion stops us from hearing other perspectives, and this limits our learning. Practice true curiosity by simply stopping and listening more.

2. *Listen to learn*—Think about the way in which you are listening. Remember Berger's listening model, and consider how often you are assuming you know the right answer and are listening with that mindset. Listen to understand, not to reply. Listen—and question—from a position of curiosity instead of trying to fix the situation or share your views.

3. *Hold curiosity conversations*—Hollywood producer Brian Grazer schedules monthly conversations with people who interest him, solely for the purpose of understanding more about what makes them tick and to broaden his own perspectives. Grazer, who won an Oscar for the film *A Beautiful Mind*, said that he does his homework before these meetings and tries to bring something meaningful to each conversation without connecting it to an ongoing project or piece of work. In an interview with *AARP: The Magazine*, Grazer said the key is asking real, genuine questions. "If you keep doing that and start creating a constellation of dots in the world you're living in, they'll connect and change your life. They'll offer you opportunities you never thought existed. They'll help you find purpose."[64]

4 *Say "yet"*—Start adding *yet* to the end of sentences that start "I don't know how to . . ." or "I'm not good at . . ." This simple change helps you to move from a fixed to growth mindset and overcome limiting beliefs that may hold you back or stop you from learning new skills. You can both practice this yourself as a leader and encourage your colleagues and employees to do the same.

5 *Keep a rethinking scorecard*—Keep track of how much input you get or how many times you "rethink" before making key decisions. One way to do this is to create what organizational psychologist Adam Grant calls a "rethinking scorecard," where you record how many times you reconsider your decisions before you finalize them.[65] This reflection helps you stay more open and flexible, countering our tendency as humans to jump to solutions too quickly.

In our fast-paced and complex world, we can all benefit from taking on a beginner's mindset. When we open ourselves to greater curiosity and flexibility, we achieve more success and have a greater impact on our business, those around us, and broader society. This openness also fosters diversity and inclusion, which we'll explore in chapter 5.

Harnessing Diverse Thinking

Because being inclusive and overcoming bias can help us be more innovative

REFLECTION

What biases do you have, and how might they be holding you back?

"Until the lion learns to write, every story will glorify the hunter."

—African proverb

For much of my early career, I worked in the technology industry. The many hours I spent in conference rooms as the only female voice gave me plenty of opportunities to reflect on the bias created when diverse perspectives aren't heard. But it isn't only female voices that our conference tables and Zoom calls are missing. Other voices are also silenced.

The challenges around diversity, equity, and inclusion are far reaching, and it's hard to consider the topic of inclusion without recognizing the wider social-justice issues surrounding it. Culturally we are having rich and sometimes difficult conversations about diversity in society and organizations worldwide. These conversations are about topics such as race, ethnicity, gender, sexual orientation, and disability in a world that continues to center around the straight, able-bodied, white, male experience.

Research consistently tells us that increasing diversity across as many dimensions as possible leads to stronger business results. Diversity across teams, leadership, and organizations results in more innovation, more creativity, more resourcefulness—and more profitability. A recent study by the consulting firm McKinsey showed that companies with greater gender diversity on their executive teams were 25 percent more likely to experience above-average profitability. The same study found that companies where executive teams were more culturally and ethnically diverse were 36 percent more likely to see better-than-average profits.[66]

While most employees and leaders know this truth, we are slow to create change. Despite seeing the data that shows the value of diversity, we tend to hire people like ourselves—and the corporate c-suite is typically white and male. As of January 2021, white people still occupied 92.6 percent of Fortune 500 CEO positions,[67] and in July 2022, men represented 95 percent of those roles.[68]

I know and fully believe all this data. But as an embarrassing case in point, I look at my own organization's team makeup, which over the past eight years has been predominantly white and female. As I am a white female founder, this may not come as a surprise, even if it is a disappointment, and it's something we are addressing proactively.

This topic merits full books of its own, and I continue to learn myself how to understand and embrace diversity in all of its dimensions. For the purposes of this chapter, we will focus on harnessing diverse thinking. As a step toward developing a leadership style that embraces inclusion and resourcefulness, we'll explore how to create a culture that not only is open to diverse perspectives and viewpoints but also proactively seeks them out.

What Inclusion Looks Like

> *Reflection: When have you felt included? How did it feel to belong to a larger community and feel fully appreciated, valued, and heard? What was happening in this community that made you feel this way? How did the leader embody and support inclusive behaviors? And when the opposite was true and you felt on the outside or excluded, how did that feel? What behaviors were you seeing—or not seeing—that caused you to feel this way?*

When we feel we belong and are truly part of a larger team or group, it can sometimes be hard to pinpoint why. For each of us, this looks different. Some of us may respond well to open, transparent communication or shared decision-making. Others may appreciate the personal, real connections across a team that allow for common understandings. Some may want an opportunity to voice their opinion and know they've been heard. As leaders, we have a responsibility to ensure the people around us feel both welcome and included. And we have to remember that for each person, what inclusion looks like may be different.

As leaders, we have a responsibility to ensure the people around us feel both welcome and included. And we have to remember that for each person, what inclusion looks like may be different.

When we think about exclusion, it's even more complicated. Sometimes we may feel excluded because of subtle behaviors that simply aren't inclusive. But other times it may be due to micro-aggressions, neglect, explicit bullying, or abuse.

According to the nonprofit Catalyst,

which supports organizations to build supportive workplaces for women, employees reported feeling included when they experienced a sense of both

1 *Uniqueness*—a feeling of being recognized and valued for their specific qualities and contributions, and

2 *Belonging*—a feeling of being welcomed and valued for who they are.

In contrast, when employees experienced a sense of exclusion, they felt both

1 Devalued, dismissed, or even ignored for their uniqueness, and

2 Like outsiders because of their differences.[69]

To be inclusive leaders, we need to create a culture that provides a safe space for everyone. But that's not enough in itself. If we want to harness diverse thinking and really overcome our biases, we also need to ensure the people around us have a wide range of backgrounds, perspectives, and experiences. One way to explore this is to consider whom you'd include in your *trusted circle*, both within and outside of work.

Increasing the range of voices around you really makes a difference— right through to business results. Inclusion increases your resourcefulness and leads to greater creativity and innovation.

Increasing the range of voices around you really makes a difference— right through to business results.

EXERCISE

Your Trusted Circle

Use this exercise to reflect on the characteristics of your trusted circle:

1 Start by making a list of ten people you most trust. These might be family members, friends, or colleagues.

2 Once you've made this list, consider how similar they are to you against a wide range of attributes. While you could include many other criteria, here is a list to start with:

- *Age*
- *Gender*
- *Nationality*
- *Language*
- *Marital status*
- *Race/ethnicity*
- *Disability*
- *Sexual orientation*
- *Religion*
- *Professional background*

3 Explore this further: How are your ten similar, and where are they diverse? What is the impact of this? If you are like most people, you will find your ten people are surprisingly similar to one another. We gravitate toward people who are like us—in background (whether cultural, ethnic, or racial) as well as in attitude and leadership style. If you limit who is in your circle, then it means that the sort of perspectives you're hearing and the scope of creativity are limited as well.

4 Looking at your list, how can you make a concerted effort to proactively seek out a broader set of voices?

Getting Close

Often, we find that the people in our trusted circle hold similar values to ours as shared values create a basis of trust. While this can create a strong foundation for a relationship, it also leads to our circle being quite small.

A challenge is how we include people in our circle who have

different values from us and who bring different points of view because we know that expanding this range of perspectives helps us come up with better solutions, new perspectives, and deeper insights. In *Braving the Wilderness*, one of Brené Brown's many powerful books, she included a chapter called "People Are Hard to Hate Close Up. Move In."[70] That sentiment is both memorable and true.

Do you have an aunt or uncle, cousin, or sister whom you love dearly but who holds completely different political views from yours? Or do you have friends whom you spent years playing alongside as children who have entirely different values from you? Brown reminds us that we can overcome these differences and expand our circle by getting close enough to others to understand their underlying intentions. It requires courage to get close and have hard conversations, but only through these conversations can we find common ground, establish real connections, and even change some minds.

> *Reflection: Think of a time when you've had really strong feelings around a divisive or controversial topic. What was at the heart of the matter for you? What truly mattered to those you disagreed with?*

When we deliberately try to engage with someone who's different from us, we broaden our perspectives. This has a ripple effect that extends past this one connection, as each person brings their own circle of influence. So if your connection is diverse to you, their circle of influence probably will be as well. However—this practice of "engaging with the enemy" is far easier said than done.

Overcoming Polarized Perspectives

Polarization is prevalent in many parts of the world, and it is exacerbated by social media.[71] In the United States, a poll by Fox News found that 81 percent of registered voters were extremely or very concerned about polarization,[72] and research by the American website FiveThirtyEight found that nearly 30 percent of Americans consider political polarization one of the country's most pressing issues (behind inflation and crime).[73] Similarly in Europe, polarization has been on the rise since the 1960s but has been at a metaphorical boiling point since the 1990s.[74] Unfortunately, these polarized perspectives have an impact on all parts of life including the workplace.

A starting point for reducing polarization and being more inclusive is listening. As author Ursula K. Le Guin wrote, "Listening is not a reaction, it is a connection. Listening to a conversation or a story, we don't so much respond as join in—become part of the action."[75] To support this, researchers and academics from MIT Sloan School of Management and Colorado College developed a powerful "Listening Challenge" to help people overcome conflict and communicate more effectively with those who hold diverse viewpoints.

It's important to remember that you can be inclusive without agreeing. You can "move in" without compromising your own values. There is value in listening to another person's perspective without saying you agree. Just listening can be very informative.

As the Listening Challenge creators explained, listening doesn't mean you have to become fully aligned or back down from your own beliefs. "It means we try to understand what other people really think, and why they act the way they do. No one can lose from greater understanding."[76]

While the Listening Challenge exists as a broader initiative, there are four key steps[77] that leaders can use to encourage more inclusive conversations:

1 *Identify each person's point of view and the value of their perspective*—In many creative processes, such as design thinking, customer journey mapping, or persona creation, teams take time to "empathize" or immerse themselves in understanding a user's perspective before designing solutions. This step is similar and can be applied to a colleague, family member, or friend. It not only helps you appreciate the value of another person's perspectives but also allows you to reflect more deeply on your own beliefs.

2 *Align around a shared purpose or goal*—Despite our differences, we often share some common goals with those around us. This shared purpose might be an organizational mission or vision, or it might be a desire to maintain a relationship. Getting clarity and agreement around where

There is value in listening to another person's perspective without saying you agree. Just listening can be very informative.

you are aligned can help to set the stage for a better, more inclusive conversation.

3 *Reflect more critically on your own views*—When we look deeply at our own held beliefs, we can often see the cracks in our arguments. Consider the weaknesses in your own positions and explore what you appreciate about the other person's point of view. How might you behave if you had someone else's experience? What are the positive points in others' views?

4 *Create solutions that everyone is likely to adopt*—Finally, with the previous steps as context, you are well positioned to look for common ground and explore innovative solutions that meet the needs of both parties. According to one of the creators of the Listening Challenge, Kate Isaacs from MIT Sloan School of Management, "It's the shift away from negotiating about people's positions on an issue and stepping back to understand their underlying fears and wants. And then creating solutions with their deeper interests in mind."

Becoming More Resourceful

Taking these listening steps is one way to help us to expand our perspectives, which is necessary if we want to enhance our resourcefulness. An important foundation to social leadership, resourcefulness is about seeing patterns, finding new connections, and then identifying novel or breakthrough solutions from that data.

Part of being resourceful is the ability to intentionally break away from established patterns to look at information in new ways. With the world moving at record pace, this ability to learn from a broad range of experiences, make new connections, and uncover fresh creative insights becomes increasingly important.

In *Range*, author David Epstein turned on its head the common belief that specialization is the only route to success. He went as far as to say that people who are generalists, think broadly, and embrace diverse experiences are those best primed to succeed.[78] Especially in a world where technology and AI move into domains once occupied by experts, there is value in honing skills in resourcefulness and inclusion and learning to find connections between what were once distinct domains.

Being inclusive and resourceful allows us to overcome our inherent bias and start seeing things from different people's perspectives.

Bryan Nixon said that at TASIS England school, they deliberately form diverse teams to stimulate this resourcefulness and get greater innovation and learning. "We very seldom work in isolation. We always work in little collaborative teams. And the reason for that is in these collaborative teams you get perspectives and insights that can be different from yours. If we all think the same, we don't learn anything."[79] Being resourceful leads to greater innovation and greater creativity. When we can harness the diversity of thought that comes from being resourceful and being innovative, we can achieve breakthroughs.

We need this diversity of thought to counter the limitations of working alone. We naturally all see things from our own perspective, based on our lived experience. When I was a child, I had a book in my library that told a parable of some blind men who came across an elephant for the first time. Each blind man tried to learn about the elephant based on feeling a different part of its body and then described it to the others based on this limited frame of reference. The one near the trunk thought it was like a snake, while the one near a leg believed it to be more like a tree. While my story had a congenial ending, in some versions of this parable, the men don't believe each other, end up suspicious that the others in the group are lying, and come to blows.

The moral is that as humans, we have a tendency to believe that what we experience is the only real truth. Despite our own limited, subjective exposure, we ignore other perspectives that may be equally valid.

In this story, as in life, no one perspective is necessarily right or wrong. It's just that each is from one person's individual viewpoint. Being inclusive and resourceful allows us to overcome our inherent bias and start seeing things from different people's perspectives.

Cognitive Bias

I often get questions about the relationship between biases and values. As I've alluded to, they are connected. Both your values and your past experiences shape your way of looking at the world, and that can create bias. This is noticeable in the workplace. For example, you might value face-to-face interaction and create a policy around working full-time in the office. But this could cause some of your employees who value working remotely to feel disgruntled or excluded.

All of us suffer from bias—both conscious and unconscious—which can hold us back from being as inclusive as we might be. *Cognitive bias* is the tendency of our brains to simplify decision-making by filtering information through our personal experience and preferences.[80]

We come by this bias naturally. Making connections—or recognizing patterns—is one of our brain's specializations.[81] Our brains are wired to make fast, intuitive decisions when needed, allowing us to survive threatening situations and deal with the sheer magnitude of data thrown our way. To accomplish this, we look for patterns and connections to what we have already experienced. While this can be highly beneficial in many circumstances, it can also lead to errors in our judgment. These errors might be caused by us having too much or too little information, or may occur when we need to make decisions quickly.

The result is bias.

Bias exists in all of us, and it constrains how we view situations, solve problems, and think through solutions. While there are over 150 unique cognitive biases,[82] let's look at just a few that impact our ability to be resourceful and inclusive.

Affinity Bias: We Prefer Those Who Are Like Us

We have a natural unconscious bias to be attracted to people who are similar to us. Called an *affinity bias*, this impacts our trusted circles as previously discussed, and it affects whom we choose to hire, befriend, and work with.

One organization doing innovative work around reducing affinity bias (and stereotypes, too, which we'll discuss next) is the Human

Library. A nonprofit learning platform that started its work in 2000, the Human Library hosts real, personal conversations between people to break down barriers and challenge stereotypes.[83] They create virtual and in-person spaces where you can "borrow" a human being—sort of like a book from a traditional library—and talk to them about a challenging topic. According to founder Ronni Abergel, they encourage challenging questions and dialogue around topics that normally aren't discussed, with real people who have direct experience. The Human Library's "human books" include people who are deafblind, bipolar, homeless, alcoholic, refugee, Muslim, or have been sexually abused, among others. The Human Library says its platform is a "chance to unjudge someone."

Reflection: What would it mean for you to "unjudge" someone?

Having access to a space for a real conversation about something we might have previously avoided helps to broaden our perspective around whom to include in our networks and communities.

Selecting a Human Book

Imagine you had an opportunity to have a conversation with one of the books in the Human Library. Make a short list of people you'd like to speak with. What experiences do you feel judgmental of or feel you don't understand well?

Once you've made your short list, select one of the people and write a list of at least five questions you'd like to ask if you were given an opportunity to have a conversation. Try to dig deep and write down the real questions that you are holding.

Then reflect on the questions you've listed. What do these questions tell you? What assumptions are you making? Beyond contacting the Human Library, how might you educate yourself further about the experience or situation you selected?

EXERCISE

Stereotyping Bias: We Tend to Discard Specifics and Form Generalities

Stereotyping is our tendency to create generalized beliefs about a certain category of people. Or, as author and activist Chimamanda Ngozi Adichie put it, "the single story creates stereotypes, and the problem with stereotypes is not that they are untrue, but that they are incomplete. They make one story become the only story."[84]

EXERCISE

"I Am; I Am Not"

To help people think about stereotyping differently, Stonehill College has developed a useful self-reflection exercise.[85] Write down as many statements as you honestly can that complete this sentence:

I am _____, but I am not _____.

When I last practiced this exercise, it made me acknowledge a number of stereotypes that exist in the world, and I felt guilty. Here were the statements that came to mind for me:

I am a woman, but I am not a bad driver.

I am in my fifties, but I am not bad with technology.

I am a mother, but I am not "stay at home."

When I dug deeper, I realized that the guilt I felt was because on some level, I had internalized these ideas even though I didn't consciously identify with or believe them. They also represented fears that I had about how other people perceived me. Getting them out on paper made them easier for me to recognize and begin letting them go. One of my clients, leader Öztunç Özada, also found this exercise enlightening. He identified the following statements for himself:

I am a man, but I'm not a football fan.

I'm a Middle Eastern person, but I'm not Muslim.

I am an auditor, but I am not a negative person.

I am a banker, but I am not boring.

I am thirty-eight, but I am not married or with children.

When reflecting on this, he said, "I am really amazed that I have come up with this. In the back of my mind, I must have these kinds of thoughts as well, and I am affected by societal stereotypes too. I thought I was free of them, but I guess none of us are."

Spend some time considering your own statements. What do they tell you about yourself?

Confirmation Bias: We Tend to Restrict Our View to What We Already Know

Have you ever heard the saying "You're preaching to the choir"? This sums up *confirmation bias*—our tendency to favor information that supports our beliefs. Social media is especially efficient at creating bubbles or echo chambers that reinforce confirmation bias, encouraging us to listen for—and then repeat—what we want to hear. We tend to close down in the face of other points of view and instead listen to and read materials that bolster our own arguments. This obviously restricts diverse thinking and resourcefulness. The Listening Challenges steps (see page 88) can help to overcome confirmation bias.

Reflection: How often do you go out of your way to read news sources that are completely unaligned with your own views?

Attribution Bias: We Tell Simple Stories

Attribution bias is the tendency to make assumptions about a person by attributing their behavior to what we perceive about their character instead of their situation. Even though we don't know what it's like to be another person, attribution bias causes us to project our own experience onto others and can lead us to close our minds to other perspectives.

Who's the Hero?

Often by shifting our perspective or taking the time to learn more about another's situation, we can overcome attribution bias. This exercise is one you can try on anyone, at any time.

1 Think of someone whom you're really struggling to understand, professionally or personally. What are a couple of words that come to mind about them?

2 Then change your perspective and think about them as the "hero" of the story. You might consider how they might describe themselves.

3 Consider the differences between these perspectives and the tone of the words you chose.

How have your feelings about the person or situation shifted?

Coach and consultant Stephanie Parry shared her experience of attribution bias: "Once when I was at a conference, I was sitting opposite a woman who looked really down and miserable. I told myself a story that she was an unpleasant person, and that I wouldn't really want to spend any time with her. Later in the conference, I ended up sitting next to her. She gave me the most beautiful smile and said, 'I'm so glad that you sat next to me because I want to participate, but I have a really bad back and can't move.' And so that completely blew away the story that I'd been telling myself about her."[86]

Bandwagon Effect: We Like to Agree

Have you ever been in a space with a crowd of people when the fire alarm goes off? If so, think back to what happened: Did you get up and

Chapter 5

go outside? Or did you sit and wait for the alarm to stop? How did your actions align with the rest of the people who were there?

My guess is that you did what everyone else did, which is an example of the *bandwagon effect*, also known as *groupthink*. A group usually acts as a whole. If you were sitting in the room on your own and the fire alarm went off, you'd probably get up and walk out. But when there's a group, you typically do what the group does. So if nobody moves, everybody stays.

This cognitive bias has implications in the workplace and can be overcome with diversity and inclusion: the more homogeneous the group, the more likely they are to resort to groupthink, vehemently agreeing with each other and creating a feedback loop that leads to poorly considered decisions.

Reflection: Have you ever changed your mind on something to go along with the group? Why do you think you did this? What was the impact of this, negative and positive?

Take Action

Inclusivity and diversity are crucial to success in the workplace. In fact, recent research, based on mathematical modeling, demonstrates that diversity is more important than ability in group decision-making. According to Scott Page from the University of Michigan, diversity reduces the likelihood of decision-making error.[87]

Restricting our point of view only limits the perspectives and experience we have access to. Here are some ways to practice resourceful inclusivity and create more opportunities for innovation and creative thinking:

1 *Escape a cognitive bias*—Go through one of the exercises in the "Cognitive Bias" section of this chapter to understand how a bias might be impacting you. Then, work to do the opposite.

2 *Create a challenge network*—Establish a network of people who are willing to actually challenge your perspective. Talk to someone who reads a different newspaper from you, for example, or comes from a different profession or background. Practice your active listening.

3 *Find a reverse mentor*—Identify someone who is different from you and ask them to mentor you. This person may come from a different part of the business or a different generation. Maybe they are a different gender or a different race. This mentorship relationship could go both ways.

4 *Set up a walk-and-talk*—When you walk and talk to someone, you are side by side with the person instead of sitting on opposite sides of a desk. It helps to enhance focus and can be especially helpful when talking to someone who holds perspectives different from yours.

5 *Rekindle dormant ties*—Think back to people you've lost touch with and have a go at reconnecting with them, especially if they might challenge the way you think. According to organizational psychologist Adam Grant, dormant ties add a lot more value in terms of innovation and creativity than the people you normally connect with.[88]

We all deserve spaces that value diverse thinking and inclusivity so we can bring all of who we are to the table. By fostering belonging, we build closer team connections. Another important component in creating connected and supportive teams is leaning into collaboration, which is what we'll discuss in the next chapter.

Building Teams That Talk

Because transparency is a foundation for effective collaboration

REFLECTION

Think of the most effective team you have been part of. What made it effective?

"The single most important ingredient in the recipe for success is transparency because transparency builds trust."

—Denise Morrison, former president and CEO at Campbell Soup Company

So far, our focus has been on skills that you can work on individually. This chapter is a little bit different as we will explore how you engage and collaborate with the people around you. This is crucial, as leaders cannot be effective in isolation; by definition, a leader cannot exist without a group to lead! Working well with other people, therefore, is essential to your success.

A main component of collaboration is conversation. The quality of the conversations you have with your teams will directly affect your business results and your overall level of impact. According to recent research by McKinsey, improved internal communication can improve organizational productivity by as much as 25 percent.[89]

The question for us as leaders then is how to create an environment where quality conversations can take place. In our leadership workshops, this question elicits comments around establishing trust, being honest, and setting clear goals. Participants talk about gaining alignment and creating clear roles and responsibilities. These all connect back to a foundation based on transparency, which helps to build the trust needed for effective collaboration.

When leaders create a collaborative environment, there is a positive impact on the bottom line: according to a recent study, companies with high trust, where employees can collaboratively and transparently share knowledge, have stock returns that are two to three times higher than the industry average as well as turnover rates that are 50 percent lower.[90]

But if it's clear that collaboration is so important, why are so many of our businesses and organizations designed with top-down hierarchical systems where a few people at the top make all the decisions?

This way of working was developed by Frederick Taylor, who was a Quaker mechanical engineer born in the United States in 1856.[91] Taylor became a foreman in a steel factory and got frustrated by its inefficiency. He started studying the work of laborers there and developed processes to streamline production. Later known as the Father of Scientific Management, he introduced theories around consistent job roles and top-down hierarchical systems. These revolutionized the business world and are concepts that have lived on globally for over a century. From his original ideas, we got job descriptions, organizational charts, and even, inadvertently, the functionally organized, siloed approach to working that many of us recognize.

Since the Industrial Revolution, we've lived in a world dominated by Taylor's principles. But the world today is different from the one he lived in, and his top-down hierarchical systems are too heavyweight and slow for today's pace of change. Let's take a look at some areas of work where conversation and collaboration can be optimized.

Use Meetings to Check In

How many hours did you spend in meetings last week? Most people's first response to this question is "Too many!"

Meetings—whether with customers or clients, employees or coworkers—are one common space where conversations can happen. If we look at the big picture, our core objective with meetings is to create stronger business or organizational results. When I ask my clients what they have on the agenda for typical meetings, they usually talk about business reviews and status updates. Sometimes they use objectives and key results (OKRs) or key performance indicators (KPIs). They review deliverables and schedules and reassess priorities. They try to hold team members accountable, remove blockages, and meet goals. They gather data for quarterly business reviews and prepare for sales meetings. Does this sound familiar? If so, I'm not surprised. And while meetings often feel less effective than they might be, these topics are important.

Rarely do we step back and explore how we are doing as individuals, how we are working together as a team, and what members need to be most effective.

If we are doing our jobs as leaders well, we spend a lot of time talking with our teams about the work we are doing and the status of ongoing projects. All of these are important conversations that track a team's success. But rarely do we step back and explore how we are doing as individuals, how we are working together as a team, and what members need to be most effective. And this is equally essential.

Therefore, I like to start meetings and workshops I hold with a "check-in." These initial interactions, usually centered around a question, give every individual a chance to reflect on how they are feeling and share what is going on for them individually.

I once did a check-in at the start of a meeting, and one of the participants said that his wife had been diagnosed with cancer. None of us knew this was going on for him. Doing this short check-in at the beginning gave him a voice, helped us understand the context he was working within, helped us feel closer to him, and reinforced trust on the team.

Here's a more complete list of the benefits a check-in provides:

- Helps participants set distractions aside and be present
- Helps participants prepare for the meeting
- Provides collective understanding of what is going on for the team
- Gives everyone a voice, which increases their engagement
- Reinforces trust
- Helps participants feel closer to others in the meeting
- Reduces possible social threat responses, or the likelihood that someone will feel emotionally triggered
- Sets the meeting's tone

EXERCISE

Team Check-In Ideas

Before you select a check-in, it's useful to think about the context for the meeting and what your specific goals are. Here are a few questions to consider:

- What is the group size? How much time do you have?
- How well do people already know each other?
- Is it a team or a group that will work together again?

The following are a few check-in ideas that we love to use at

Be Leadership. These can be done out loud, whether in person or on-screen, and some could be adapted for a chat pane.

1 *One word*—Share one word to indicate how you are feeling today.

2 *Scale of 1 to 10*—How are you feeling on a scale of 1 to 10, and what's contributing to that?

3 *Draw an emoji*—Draw a smiley/emoji/picture to describe how you feel today and hold it up when asked.

4 *Rose, thorn, bud*—What is one thing you're feeling happy about (rose), one challenge or concern (thorn), and one thing you're looking forward to (bud)?

5 *Traffic light*—What is your traffic light color (red = stressed, distracted, anxious; yellow = somewhat distracted or pressured; green = fully present, ready to go)? What's contributing to that? What support do you need?

6 *Arm lever*—Cross your arms and use your top arm as a lever to indicate your energy level. Straight up and down is high energy; flat is low energy.

7 *Show-and-tell*—Choose an item, either found in real time if working virtually or selected in advance, and share why you selected it based on these prompts:

- *Something that represents how you're showing up today*
- *Something that is meaningful to you*
- *Something gifted to you by someone important in your life*

Create a Team That Talks by Listening

In the business world, *transparency* is centered on the sharing of data, information, and ideas, but there's an important connection between transparency and authenticity. In our social leadership framework, *authenticity* is about representing ourselves in a way that is congruent with our values or sharing our true selves. Authenticity creates a foundation for better and easier data sharing. When relationships between team members are strong, we are more likely to be open and clear in our communication and sharing of progress, both positive and negative.

By our definition, transparent leaders reduce threat and uncertainty in their organizations by being as clear as possible with information and sharing what is real and true. Further, they accept and admit their mistakes, showing others that they should feel safe to do so as well. They put an emphasis on openness and share ideas in the early stages to increase inclusivity and trust by engaging people and getting input before plans are final.

In this hugely turbulent world, transparency can create needed certainty for our employees and colleagues, reducing the threat response they may feel around rapid change and ambiguity. If you want to be a transparent leader, real transparency starts with listening. If you share without also giving people a voice, you are not creating genuine dialogue.

Real transparency starts with listening. If you share without also giving people a voice, you are not creating genuine dialogue.

Without listening, it's impossible to have a two-way conversation. In *Talk, Inc.*, authors Boris Groysberg and Michael Slind shared perspectives on how real discussion can be used to power an organization. They wrote, "When a leader starts to treat listening to employees as no less important than speaking to them, the lines of communication between the top and bottom of an organization become a set of arrows that point up as well as down."[92]

One company that excels at this is Red Hat. An IBM subsidiary and open-source software company, Red Hat uses a transparent process of decision-making that former CEO Jim Whitehurst detailed in the book *The Open Organization*. This process includes both inclusive listening and spirited conversation where the best ideas win, no matter their source. While Whitehurst acknowledged that this approach leads to friction and sometimes even conflict, he also argued that it ultimately results in faster and better results. "The more transparent you make the decision-making process, the more effectively you can turn those decisions into real actions that everyone can engage in," he said.[93]

While the early stages of decision-making can take longer, the solutioning is faster and higher quality. Whitehurst explained, "We strive for change management to happen during the decision-making process, not during execution. We've learned that to bring about changes, it's not enough to simply sell our associates on a decision after it's been made."[94] In other words, earlier listening and input lead to better outcomes and collaboration.

Groysberg and Slind build on this idea by sharing four key elements that are needed in conversation for our communication to lead to greater collaboration: intimacy, interactivity, inclusion, and intentionality. Let's take a look at each.

Intimacy

Don't let this word throw you. What *intimacy* means in this context is bridging the gap between you and the people you work with or "building trust through talk."[95] We can create more intimate (as opposed to distant) communication by meeting in smaller groups and using skills in listening and authenticity to start conversations that are more real. Here are a few ideas on how you might go about this:

- Skip-level meetings where you meet people above or below you in your management chain who aren't your immediate manager or direct reports
- Recurring listening sessions or councils that bring together diverse stakeholders
- Coffee mornings
- Peer mentoring programs
- Intentional walks through the office corridors to create connections

At Be Leadership, we create this type of intimacy across our team despite working virtually. One example of this is what we call #BeBuddies. Each January, those who sign up for the program agree to give and receive non-monetary gifts and support at least once per week throughout the month. Over the years, team members have shared music, jokes, photos, or quotes and have supported each other with coaching, peer mentoring, or virtual coffees. Not only does this help make for a nicer start to the year; it also helps us get to know each other at a different, more personal level.

Interactivity

By its definition, dialogue is not one person speaking. Conversation is a give-and-take and requires skills in both talking and listening. We need the exchange of ideas to get the benefits from talking, and this means cultivating our skills in questioning, active listening, and engaging others. In the words of Groysberg and Slind, "The sound of one person talking, whatever else it may be, is not a conversation."[96]

At a recent Be Leadership workshop, leader Mauro Barcellos described the importance of interactivity. He said it all starts with listening to team members. "As soon as we start to listen, we should try to understand them. Because if they don't feel understood, it's probably going to be very difficult to make them talk."

Reflection: When you are in a conversation, what percentage of the time do you spend listening?

Inclusion

We've covered this in the previous chapter, but it's worth mentioning in this context. When it's done well, conversation gives everyone an opportunity to have an equal voice. This is easier said than done, yet companies and organizations that do this well reap the benefits. Take for instance the film studio Pixar, which, like Red Hat, sees innovation and creativity emerge from inclusive decision-making.

Ed Catmull, one of Pixar's cofounders, said, "A hallmark of a healthy creative culture is that people feel free to share ideas, opinions, and criticisms."[97] While this can lead to the same friction Whitehurst reflected on, the overall impact of this inclusion is positive: "There is no doubt our decision-making is better if we are able to draw on the collective knowledge and unvarnished opinions of the group," Catmull said.

Bryan Nixon said the same of his work with the teachers and staff at TASIS England school, where they work in small collaborative teams in order to hear and incorporate diverse perspectives. "If we all think the same, we don't learn anything," Nixon said. "I like to surround myself with people who can think differently, who can challenge me, who are not afraid to tell me that I'm going down a dark alley or I'm doing something wrong. It's really important to have that level of creative dissonance."[98]

Intentionality

As you work to expand and strengthen conversations through intimacy, interactivity, and inclusion, it's important to be clear on their intention, or overarching purpose. Groysberg and Slind stressed that organizational conversations need to contribute to developing a collective understanding of a company's strategic objectives.[99]

At TASIS, focus is given to communication and transparency, but not at the expense of this intentionality.[100] Nixon talked about the attention he has given to centering the organization around its mission statement to help it respond well in times of uncertainty. "Change is inevitable, and it is part of our daily lives," he said. "But there are still things that hold true. One of the first things I do when I come into a school is work with the community to help them truly understand who they are. Whether the school is facing a challenging time with regulatory bodies or a pandemic or any other situation, our mission statement is our anchor."

Reflection: Think of a team that you work with and the communications you have with them. What is your anchor?

Recognize the Limits of Transparency

If we assume those four elements are present and appropriate conversations are starting to happen across the organization, when should we recognize transparency's limits? What does it mean to be *too* transparent? For all that it does to promote trust and allow for shared learning, too much of it can be counterproductive. Like many leadership skills, when overplayed, transparency no longer provides the intended benefits.

In England, the train companies have punctuality policies that require them to be transparent about the specific reasons trains are running late or are canceled. The most common cause of delay is a signaling failure, but it is not surprising to hear announcements like "We are sorry for the delay to this train. The bathroom in car four is flooded." Or "The previous train has yet to leave the station." Or even more personal: "The driver is late."

I once was on a train heading into London, and an announcement was made that said, "We apologize for the delay. The driver is having an argument with the guard." Everyone around me rolled their eyes in frustration. Though the intention of this transparency was to create higher levels of consumer confidence, the reaction of my fellow riders illustrates that transparency alone doesn't always lead to higher levels of trust. Sharing the details of the problem but no information around a solution doesn't necessarily create improvements.

By returning to the four key elements of intimacy, interactivity, inclusion, and intentionality, you can establish appropriate transparency that helps to create a culture of trust.

What Do You Share?

When deciding what to share with employees, ask yourself these questions:

- What is the intent behind sharing this information?

- Is this information relevant to all employees?

- Does knowing this information benefit them in some way?

- Is it essential for their jobs?

- Will it help to develop richer relationships on the team?

- Is it fact, or is it opinion or rumor?

- Is there room for misinterpretation?

- What might be the unintended consequences of sharing this?

Craft Team Agreements

One of the best ways to increase a team's effectiveness is to have an open conversation about how that team wants to work together and what each individual on the team needs to be most successful. In some organizations, hybrid working is now the norm, and it creates new challenges around collaboration.

American-headquartered cloud-based software company Salesforce believes that success comes from working from anywhere, which doesn't necessarily mean in an office. Salesforce has been recognized as a company leading the way in embracing hybrid, and data collected from their employees showed that 80 percent want a connection to the office but don't necessarily need it every day, and 75 percent want some flexibility in how and where they work.[101]

Not everyone wants to be virtual; in fact, in this research, younger workers had a stronger preference for working in the office. These same trends are seen in research performed in other sectors and markets. Having an open and transparent conversation about what each of us needs from our workplace helps to sow the seeds for greater trust and stronger collaboration. This is particularly true as we change how we work beyond the pandemic.

At Salesforce, employees are given a choice of three ways of working:

- Office-flexible—Working in the office one to three days a week (on average) and the rest remotely

- Home-based—Working remotely 100 percent of the time

- Office-based—Working in the office 100 percent of the time

At a conference held by the World Institute for Action Learning, Senior Vice President Angela McKenna shared the fact that their "success from anywhere" strategy relies on what they call *flex team agreements*.[102] These agreements are created collaboratively by teams to discuss and decide how, when, and where they will work, including behaviors they want to see in their collaboration, when they will be in the office, and what types of work they do at home. These conversations are centered around both mechanics and dynamics—or, put another way, what they need to do to collaborate well and how they want to behave together.

While Salesforce introduced these team agreements to support hybrid work, the structure can be used for teams working in other contexts too. If you are reading this and realize that you are on a team that hasn't spent much time recently discussing how, when, or where everyone works, it's not too late.

The first step is to schedule some dedicated time for a conversation around both mechanics and dynamics, asking people to reflect in advance on how they feel the team is working together, what is going well, and what could be even better. Then, when the team is together, you can spend a few minutes looking back at what's already working that you want to retain and what you can change to increase the team's effectiveness. Let's take a closer look.

Mechanics

Team mechanics are the processes and structures that the team members use to work together. These include logistics like frequency, duration, and location (as well as technology platforms), but also may incorporate more-detailed mechanics.

For example, some of my clients rely on Monday stand-ups, where they check in with each other briefly each Monday and deliberately remain standing to ensure the meeting stays short and efficient. Other companies have a guideline that documents must be shared and read ahead of meetings. This creates an assumption that everyone has the same information coming into the conversation, so the meeting can be spent on the details. For some leaders, using frameworks or models like OGSM (objectives, goals, strategies, measures) or RACI (establishing who is responsible, accountable, consulted, and informed) can help to ensure the team is aligned.

Establishing Norms around Processes and Structures

Prepare your team for a conversation around mechanics by sending out these powerful questions in advance. Give the team members an opportunity to think about what they each need individually before bringing the group together to draft an agreement:

- How often should the team meet?

- Should our meetings be in person, virtual, or hybrid?

- Who should be there?

- What should be on the agenda?

- Who should lead the meetings?

- When and how long should team meetings be?

- How will we share information?

- How will we keep track of our decisions and progress?

- How will people be held accountable?

Dynamics

When team agreements or charters do exist, they often cover mechanics but neglect the dynamics. You won't be surprised to hear I think the dynamics of a team are equally, if not more, important to cover in these agreements.

The dynamics side of the agreement is all about how we engage with each other: What behaviors do we want to demonstrate within our team to be most successful? This could be asking more open questions. It could be treating others with respect or assuming noble intent. It could be that we give everyone an opportunity to have an equal voice. It's important that the whole team is involved in establishing the norms that are desired.

Aligning around Team Behaviors

Share these questions for individual reflection ahead of a conversation around team dynamics:

- What behaviors do we most want to see on our team?

- What does participation in the team mean to us?

- How should we inform each other if we can't attend?

- How should we deal with lateness or absence?

- How can we encourage strong participation?

- How do we make decisions?

- How should we handle conflict?

- How do we hold ourselves accountable to this agreement?

During your team's conversation, draft an agreement. Then, be sure to ask for feedback from all team members before finalizing. Remember that the goal with a team agreement isn't that you set the rules and present them to your team as a fait accompli. The conversation around this agreement is as important as the norms you commit to together. When your team sets the rules, they are more likely to hold each other and you accountable to them.

The goal with a team agreement isn't that you set the rules and present them to your team as a fait accompli. The conversation around this agreement is as important as the norms you commit to together.

Take Action

Appropriate transparency creates trust, which fosters better communication, which leads to stronger collaboration.

Along with adding meeting check-ins (page 105) and creating team agreements (page 112), here are some more key practical ideas you can adopt if you want to increase transparency and trust with those you lead:

1 *Plan non-work-related time together as a team*—Remember that for the greatest business impact, we need to spend time on both relationships (creating real connections) and tasks (getting the job done). Spending unstructured or non-work-related time together as a team leads to a greater ability to work through misunderstandings or challenges you might face while working together.

2 *Schedule listening sessions*—Plan a series of meetings with no agenda other than hearing people's thoughts, views, and feelings. Consider involving people whom you don't speak to as often or stakeholders who are really important to your team and whom you don't collaborate as closely with. Gather a diverse set of perspectives. Remember, these sessions are not for sharing your own views but rather opportunities to simply listen and say thank you.

3 *Use 10×10×10 communication*—There is a rule that says that you need to say things ten times in ten different ways for people to retain 10 percent.[103] Think about how you are communicating, and try to step up the number of times you share key messages with your team.

4 *Say what needs to be said*—Real conversations can be difficult to have, especially if there is potential conflict involved. As a leader, you need to have the courage to address issues as they arise. Be ready to be unpopular and know that what you are doing is best for the business. Letting these things fester beneath the surface will only cause bigger issues later.

5 *Share context*—Take the time to explain the reasoning behind decisions and not just the decision itself. This allows people to understand your thought processes and increases the likelihood they will align behind the decisions made.

As a leader, you have an opportunity to create teams who trust one another and have high-quality collaboration and conversations. This leaves more space for you to focus on what matters most and build accountability, which is what we'll discuss in chapter 7.

Focusing on Accountability

Because focusing on
what matters most
increases accountability

REFLECTION

*How often do you feel able
to focus on just one thing?*

"What matters is now, this moment, and your willingness to see this moment for what it is, accept it, forgive the past, take responsibility, and move forward."

—Oprah Winfrey, media mogul

I n 2017, researchers at the University of Texas at Austin ran a study looking at the effect our mobile phones have on our ability to concentrate and perform cognitive tasks. I remember reading about it when it came out because I found the results so surprising, and yet at the same time, so expected.

In this experiment, the researchers asked some people to sit at a computer and take a few tests that required concentration and focus. One-third of the participants were asked to leave their phones outside the room. Those in the second group were asked to place them on the desk next to them, face down. Those in the final group were asked to put their phones in their pockets or personal bag. All were asked to set their phones to silent.

When the results of the test were tallied, the participants with their phones in another room significantly outperformed those with their phones next to them on the desk, and they also slightly outperformed those who had put their phones in their pocket or bag.

The findings suggested that having a phone in reach—even if it's off—impacts our ability to focus and be present and has a negative impact on our cognitive functioning.[104]

Technology is a constant in our lives today, and it brings distractions alongside its benefits. We all must find ways to remain *present* and *accountable* despite this challenge. In this chapter, you'll learn tips to focus on the things that matter to enhance your accountability and effectiveness, especially in the workplace, but also more broadly.

Being Present

Across the thousands of leaders who have taken Be Leadership's social leadership self-assessment, *presence* has come up most often as an area people feel needs development. This is not surprising as it's not just our phones that steal our attention—we are surrounded by potential distractions: from wars, global pandemics, climate change, and cost-of-living crises to technology and social media. All result in our having more complex lives and more demands on our time and attention, which makes it difficult to stay focused on the present moment.

Being present is about focusing on one thing at a time. Those who do it successfully avoid distractions and listen actively. These leaders

Being present is about focusing on one thing at a time.

understand the value of work-life balance and encourage their employees to take time for themselves as well. They demonstrate through their body language that they are fully engaged. When we are present as leaders, we ask better, more relevant questions; we are able to build on what's been said more effectively; and we can more appropriately bring emotion into our replies.

Being in the present moment helps us to be connected with not just ourselves, but the people and world around us too.

This is easier said than done, though. I talk to people every week who struggle to stay focused. I have issues with this myself—just twenty minutes ago I stopped writing to look up some research. While I was searching for what I needed, I "quickly" checked my email and then my phone messages. What should have taken me two minutes took me a quarter of an hour.

One of the challenges of remaining focused is the fact that we all have high-priority communications coming at us all day, every day. The proliferation of messaging applications and our seeming inability to disconnect make this even more difficult. What might have once been a string of people waiting outside our door is now dozens or often hundreds of messages bombarding us from multiple applications and devices.

All these messages and tasks can feel equally critical, but if we as leaders are unable to find time for the more strategic and important parts of our roles, our success in the operational realm can block overall development. Being present and focusing on the right things can increase our effectiveness as social leaders. Let's take a look at a couple of strategies you can apply right away to help you make the most of your time.

The Eisenhower Matrix

One tool that helps with organizing tasks so you can prioritize more effectively is the Eisenhower Matrix. This tool, developed by author Stephen Covey, categorizes tasks into four types, ensuring you reflect carefully on importance and urgency:[105]

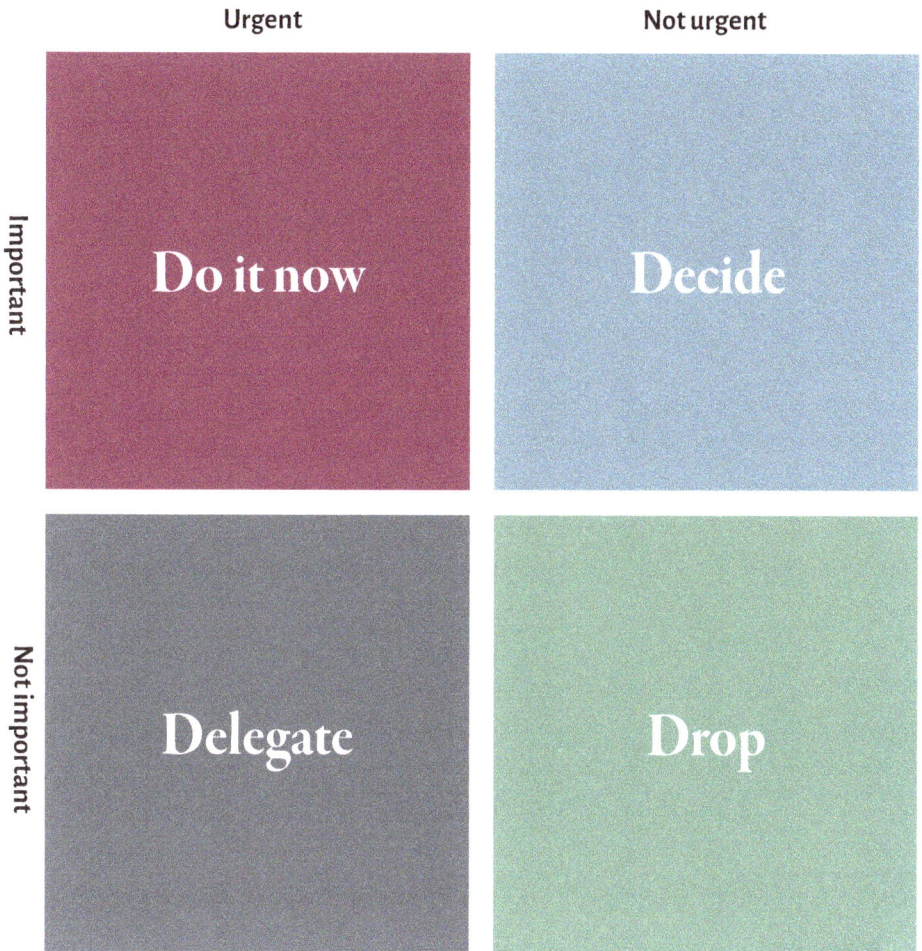

	Urgent	Not urgent
Important	Do it now	Decide
Not important	Delegate	Drop

1 Things to tackle first

2 Things to schedule time for later

3 Things to delegate

4 Things to drop or disregard

The model is named after thirty-fourth US president Dwight D. Eisenhower, who credited a former university president in 1954 when he said, "I have two kinds of problems, the urgent and the important. The urgent are not important, and the important are never urgent."[106]

While they seem similar and often can be confused in our minds as we go through our days, there is a distinction between the concepts of urgency and importance:

- **Urgent** tasks demand immediate action or attention. They are often driven by external factors or deadlines, and there can be at least a sense that if they are not accomplished, there will be negative repercussions.

  Examples of urgent tasks in the workplace might include responding to a last-minute query, finishing a project with a short deadline, or fixing an embarrassing public error. In our personal lives, urgent tasks may include paying a bill that is overdue, scheduling a doctor's appointment for an injury, or picking up a child who missed a school bus.

- **Important** tasks help you achieve your long-term goals or relate to your own personal priorities. While urgency is often externally dictated, a task's importance is determined by you. Important tasks may not require immediate attention, but they matter.

  Examples of important tasks may include networking, informational interviews to support career planning, or writing a strategy document. They can also include completing routine chores or maintenance. In our personal lives, important tasks can include fitness classes or exercise, maintaining friendships, or planning a holiday with family.

Once you know how to distinguish between urgency and importance, you can begin separating your tasks into the four quadrants of the Eisenhower Matrix.

Important and Urgent

Do it now—Tasks should be done immediately and personally
A task that is urgent and important requires immediate action. These tasks typically have a tight deadline and have consequences

if not addressed. We often can't plan for urgent and important tasks because they only show up at the last minute. Spending too much of our time in this quadrant, however, can lead to burnout.

You can reduce the stress that comes from this quadrant by avoiding procrastination and planning windows in your schedule to handle these types of unexpected demands.

Reflection: Where are you spending your time? How are you planning for the important and urgent tasks that are likely to come your way each week?

Important and Not Urgent

Decide—Tasks should be scheduled and done personally
Activities that are not urgent but important are those that can help you achieve your long-term goals. It's easy to put these off because they don't have an immediate deadline, but if they are not given attention, they can have a large impact on your longer-term success and satisfaction.

Focusing attention on tasks in this quadrant can actually reduce the number of urgent tasks you face. For example, if you exercise and go to the dentist for checkups, you improve your health and reduce the number of health emergencies you might face later. If you work proactively on a project, you may reduce the number of short-term deadlines you have to meet.

Reflection: What is something important but not urgent that you wish you were giving higher priority? How could you break this project down into smaller parts or milestones so you can make better progress?

One way to manage important-but-not-urgent tasks is to pre-schedule blocks of time in your calendar to give them priority. As an example of this, I set aside one week near the end of my business's fiscal year, and I hold what I call a *Think Week* (a term Bill Gates uses that I repurposed). During this week, I step outside of delivery and client-facing work, and I spend full days thinking about my business and doing strategic planning. These types of activities are incredibly hard to focus on when I'm wrapped up in day-to-day delivery, but when I block time for them, I can hold myself accountable.

Another way to prioritize important activities is to set what Jackie Yeaney calls daily or weekly *guideposts*. According to Yeaney, who worked as a chief marketing officer at software companies Tableau and Red Hat, these commitments you make with yourself can lower stress and increase your chance of success because they are preestablished, or "decisions before the decision."[107]

Some of Yeaney's guideposts included:

- I will make half of all three kids' soccer games.
- I won't work on the weekend and will be 100 percent mom and wife.
- I will make dinner at least three times a week.
- I will attend a networking event two times a month.
- I will act as a sounding board, coach, or mentor for someone at least once a week.

By creating these promises to herself, Yeaney managed to spend a better amount of time on the things that were important to her: "The magic I found was that I didn't have to torture myself every day with trying to make appropriate trade-offs. I had already decided!"[108]

Unimportant and Urgent

Delegate—Tasks should be reprioritized or assigned to others
Tasks that are urgent but not actually important are often described as "busywork." These are activities that others might deem essential but don't help you achieve your long-term goals. Spending too long in this quadrant can lead to dissatisfaction.

If you work in an office, this might include someone knocking on your door unexpectedly and asking for a minute of your time. While this could ultimately be classed as urgent and important for the other person, it may not meet either bar for you.

Many times, when we answer emails or respond to social media notifications or text messages, we are working in this unimportant and urgent category. We may erroneously assume the urgency of these tasks or allow others to put us under pressure to accept deadlines that are not in line with our own priorities.

Reflection: Where are you creating too much urgent pressure on yourself? Where might you release pressure and slow down a bit to make your leadership more sustainable?

For these tasks, it's worth thinking about whether you are the right person to be doing them, or who else can do them for you. If you're not able to delegate these activities, you can reduce the time they take from your day by taking the following actions:

- Asking questions of others to clarify deadlines and urgency
- Being clear around how much time you have available
- Turning off notifications on your phone and other devices
- Practicing saying no

Unimportant and Not Urgent

Drop—Tasks should be eliminated
Activities that are unimportant and not urgent are generally time wasters. These are things you are spending time on, but you are not required to do them. You may not be getting value from them yourself. You might ask why we spend time in this quadrant, but we do. Such activities can include watching television, browsing the internet, and scrolling through social media feeds.

Reflection: What are you spending time on that falls into the category of unimportant and not urgent? What value, if any, does this type of activity bring to your life? What else would you like to do instead that would bring you even more value?

You might argue that the activities I'm describing are important to you because they provide needed relaxation or downtime. If that's the case, they don't really fall into this category. But if you want to reduce the time you spend on these activities, think about what else you could be doing and the value you would get from the alternatives. Create boundaries for yourself and hold to them—if you want to watch one hour of television, watch it and then turn the TV off. You might find it's easier to hold yourself to these boundaries if you have alternative activities that you can turn to instead.

EXERCISE

Perform a Calendar Review

When you are going from meeting to meeting, crisis to crisis, it can be difficult to have awareness around how exactly you are spending your time. Try this exercise to see what you are actually getting done each day and what is distracting you from accomplishing more.

1 Select a typical day in your diary or calendar.

2 Looking at a printed or written copy of this day, take time to reflect on what you notice. Think about the feelings you have reading through this day. Consider the number of meetings, their duration, and how often you have breaks for food and movement. Are the right people in these meetings? Do you need to attend them all?

3 Notice what you are doing outside of the scheduled events. In a notebook or app, break down your entire day into hourlong increments, and then each hour, jot down the tasks you attended to in that time frame. This includes things like checking email, scrolling through social media, breaks for stretching, interruptions from employees, and so on.

4 Take a look at the information you've gathered. What is working? What is not? How do the tasks you are currently doing fit into the Eisenhower Matrix? Consider the changes you wish to make to your agenda and scheduling so you are using time efficiently.

5 A great tip is blocking some windows in your calendar to allow time for things you currently aren't getting done. Need more time to deal with urgencies that come up in the day? Create some appointments to give yourself space for that. Want focused working time to make progress on your highest priorities? Schedule time for reflection at the point in the day that works best for you. Then hold yourself accountable to take the time for what is intended.

6 As a bonus, repeat this exercise with a focus on your time before and after work to see how you can make time for what matters most in your personal life.

Pause and Reflect

Sometimes things land in our lap unexpectedly—through email, a WhatsApp message, or an unexpected phone call, for example—and we have to make quick decisions around where they fall in the important-urgent matrix. Because this rapid decision-making can be challenging, we frequently default to the easiest, but possibly least appropriate response, which is "Sure, I'll do it now."

It's worth taking a step back in these situations before you reply and considering whether this is the right approach. In her book *A Minute to Think*, Juliet Funt recommended taking just one minute to assess requests and determine their priority.

Using what she called "the Hourglass method," she suggested that we pause before responding and ask ourselves a series of questions, starting with considering our first instinct around whether we should say yes or no. She suggested that after noting this "flash response," we reflect on the motives behind this instinctual answer, what we can learn from similar past situations, and how a decision will impact us in the days and weeks ahead.[109]

Faced with this type of interruption, I recommend the following:

1 *Start with a question*—Push back on other people's urgency. When you hear "Can I have five minutes for a quick question?" or someone sends you an email for something that's

urgent, stop to consider your response instead of jumping straight in. Appropriate replies might be "How urgent is this?"; "Can this wait until our next scheduled meeting?"; or "Can you give me some context for this request so I can prioritize it correctly?" All of these will help you to establish your own priorities instead of immediately responding to the urgency of others. You will often find these types of tasks move immediately into the nonurgent and can be scheduled for a later time.

2 *Buy yourself some time*—Ask, "Can I have a few minutes/hours/days to come back to you?" Even if the request is deemed urgent, you can still ask for some time to think through the appropriate response before just saying yes and starting to take action.

3 *Reflect on what might be influencing your thinking*—As Funt suggested, consider what is underlying your flash response through questions around motive and history. These might look like: What assumptions am I making that may influence how I may respond? Am I harboring fears or worries around being liked, needed, or recognized that could be swaying my decision? This self-reflection might also explore what you can learn from past decisions you have made and how those played out.

4 *Consider the trade-offs*—We all have twenty-four hours in each day. If you say yes to this request, you likely will have to say no to something else. Are these trade-offs worth it? Being aware of this before you jump in will help you set expectations for yourself and others.

Having gone through this reflection, you will be in a better position to make a good decision around the urgency and importance of this request. Then you can craft or deliver a considered, and appropriate, response.

Accountability

Presence is closely linked with accountability. Consider this scenario: You are given the responsibility of walking a young child across a busy street. This is a task that requires a high degree of accountability. If you're doing it while texting, you can't actually act accountably because you're not present. Similarly, if you're in a one-on-one meeting with someone who works for you, you should hold yourself accountable for this meeting and focus on your employee. But if you're checking your email at the same time, there's no way that you can be accountable.

Accountability is about being answerable for your actions and being reliable. Accountable leaders hold themselves and others to a high standard, clearly delegate, and share ownership.

Accountability is about being answerable for your actions and being reliable. Accountable leaders hold themselves and others to a high standard, clearly delegate, and share ownership.

Being present and accountable are essential social leadership skills because they give us time and space to accomplish what matters most. When we stay in the present, make accountable decisions, and keep our focus on our priorities, it helps us ensure we are able to spend time on what is most aligned with our purpose. Let's go over a few ways to hone your accountability and focus.

Stop Playing the Victim

I was on a team for many years that had a problem related to accountability: The top leaders were always running fifteen minutes late. The rest of us would arrive in a conference room for a sixty-minute meeting and wait together for a quarter of the hour for the same key people to arrive. What they said as they rushed into the meeting room was nearly always the same: "Sorry, my previous meeting ran over."

By blaming their delays on their previous meetings, the tardy leaders on this team were unknowingly suffering from what's called a victim mentality.

As victims, we focus on things that are outside our control. We may distance ourselves from problems to maintain our self-esteem and shift blame to external forces and other people. When we are playing the victim, we can feel powerless and trapped.

Warning signs that we are playing the victim include the following:

- We complain.
- We get jealous.
- We shirk responsibility or blame others.
- We feel sorry for ourselves.
- We hold on to grudges.

When we overcome this victim mindset, we become more empowered and accountable. We recognize that our circumstances may not be our fault, but they are our responsibility. We see ourselves as part of a broader system and therefore recognize our role in the problem. Accountable leaders see external forces as neither good nor bad, but as challenges to overcome. Ultimately when we escape victimhood, we recognize we have a choice in how to respond, and we work to create solutions.

Here's what this looks like in practice:

- We accept responsibility.
- We are resilient.
- We are resourceful.
- We look for solutions.
- We forgive more easily.

In the case of the leadership team I worked with, we eventually decided as a group to set up a "late fee" system. Anyone who was more than five minutes late had to put some significant cash in the pot, which was eventually used for a team morale event. This lightened the mood while increasing accountability and encouraging more prompt attendance.

While the excuses we make usually seem harmless, author of *Conscious Business* Fred Kofman said that the words we use are an indicator of the mindset we hold.[110] When we use language like "Sorry, my previous meeting ran over," we are relinquishing responsibility—we are speaking as if we were passive participants in a calendar that is outside our control. If we instead choose to say, "Sorry I was late. I didn't manage my time," we take an active stance. Here are some additional examples of how you can shift your language from that of a victim to one that is more accountable:

From	To
Sorry, my previous meeting ran over.	Sorry I was late. I didn't manage my time.
Our partner hasn't responded.	We haven't chased the partner hard enough.
Customers don't get it.	We haven't demonstrated enough value.
We missed our budget target because the market was down.	We didn't forecast well enough this quarter.
It's not my fault.	I haven't found a solution yet.

The Accountability Ladder

If you are trying to make a shift and increase your accountability, it can be useful to consider where you are on the accountability ladder. This framework was popularized by Bruce Gordon, former president of the NAACP, an American civil rights organization, and it describes eight steps that one is likely to take when moving from being a powerless victim to a powerful, fully accountable leader.[111]

At the lowest levels of the ladder, where we are a complete victim, we are unaware or oblivious to our possible role in the situation, and therefore completely powerless. As we move up the ladder to positions of accountability, we become more powerful. Each step is one of increased ownership: we move from being unaware to being aware but blaming others. Then, when we start to recognize we may have a role, we find excuses. When we learn our excuses aren't completely valid, we look to dismiss our role as insignificant. As we move into positions of power, though, we begin to acknowledge the part that we are playing, take ownership, and finally find and apply solutions.

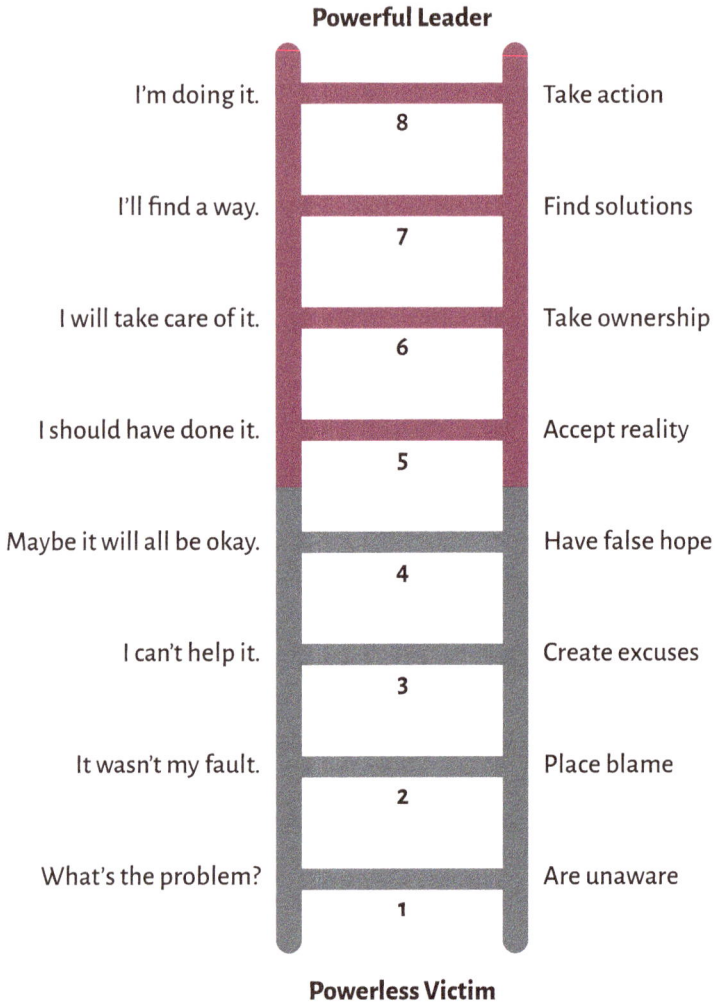

Powerful Leader

I'm doing it.	8	Take action
I'll find a way.	7	Find solutions
I will take care of it.	6	Take ownership
I should have done it.	5	Accept reality
Maybe it will all be okay.	4	Have false hope
I can't help it.	3	Create excuses
It wasn't my fault.	2	Place blame
What's the problem?	1	Are unaware

Powerless Victim

Climbing the Ladder

You can use the accountability ladder to shift your mindset more toward a position of power. Note that these same steps can be taken to support someone else with this transition:

1 Think about a recent work or personal situation that was challenging for you. What happened and what was your response?

2 Reflect carefully on the accountability ladder. Where were you on this?

3 We move from victimhood gradually through ongoing practice, and with intention. With this in mind, how might you have responded with more accountability?

4 The next time you face a challenge, reflect on how you are responding in the moment. Can you move up one rung to shift away from victimhood?

Playing the victim can feel safe and help to preserve our self-esteem because it can help us avoid being blamed or called out. But it also keeps us stuck in a frustrating situation where we neither want to accept nor take responsibility to change. We are giving up power.

As we think about holding ourselves and others accountable, we can start by paying attention to our language and our mindset. When we conquer the victim mentality, it comes with increased accountability and, possibly, risk of failure. But we can move forward with confidence if we base our self-esteem on taking responsibility and working with integrity. We can retain our self-respect and change the situation we are facing by exercising freedom of choice.

Take Action

We are living in a fast-paced world. If you sometimes feel over-whelmed and struggle to focus, you are certainly not alone. As a leader, you can be overloaded with urgent operational demands, making it hard to find the time to give thought to the bigger picture or longer-term challenges. Here are some ideas to help you develop presence and accountability:

1   *Go deviceless*—Make an agreement with yourself and those around you to put your phones away at mealtimes, during meetings, or when you are sleeping. Buy an old-fashioned alarm clock, and sleep with your mobile phone in a different room to improve your sleep quality. Increase your presence and create focus on those in the room with you during meals or meetings by setting ground rules around device usage during those times.

2   *Identify your three "big rocks"*—Get more clarity on your important and nonurgent tasks by determining what some call your "big rocks" or your three highest priorities. Write these down and put them somewhere that is visible to you. Each day evaluate what you are doing against those priorities and use the Eisenhower Matrix to shift more energy to what matters.

3   *Control your response*—You can't always control what happens to you, but you *can* decide how you respond to it. Next time something doesn't go according to plan, consider whether your reaction is one of a victim. To shift up the accountability ladder, ask yourself, *What am I able to control in this situation?* Even if all you can control is how you think and respond to the situation, that is all you need to empower your actions moving forward. Take a stance that doesn't relinquish your power.

4 *Delegate to your employees*—Social leaders have confidence in their staff. They hold them accountable by delegating responsibility. Sometimes our calendars get filled with "urgent" tasks because we struggle to let go and trust others. We convince ourselves that our skills and experience are needed to accomplish a task successfully. Try taking a step back and think about the broader context, and the impact of doing this yourself, right now.

Remember, staying present and holding yourself accountable to focusing on what really matters will increase your effectiveness as a social leader. Taking these steps will help you become more effective in managing your time and ensure you spend your days on the tasks that are most important for you. This matters even more as we move into the next chapter, where we'll focus on how we set an example and give back as leaders.

Leading by Example

Because we are more inspiring when we give back and show others the way

What kind of example did you provide today?

"When you've worked hard, and done well, and walked through that doorway of opportunity . . . you do not slam it shut behind you . . . you reach back, and you give other folks the same chances that helped you succeed."

—Michelle Obama, former American First Lady

Over the course of writing this book, I've reflected on leaders who have positively impacted my life and career. The list is long and stretches from early in my childhood through to today. I've been fortunate to learn from countless people who have helped me develop into who I am. For me, these leaders have been nothing short of inspiring.

I was inspired by my high school teacher who nearly bounced up and down in front of the classroom when she shared her passion for journalism and copywriting. My grandmother inspired me with both her strength of character and acceptance of those with different life experiences. My parents taught me consistent and lifelong lessons around inclusion and service. Recently, I've been surrounded by other people in my field who impress me with their depth of knowledge, compassion, courage, and authenticity.

Individuals make a difference in all of our lives and serve as inspiration in a variety of ways. Recent research by Mark Horwitch and Meredith Whipple Callahan at Bain & Company found that there is a wide range of characteristics leaders can demonstrate to be perceived as inspiring, and what's important is that they have one "distinguishing" strength—a skill where they are in the top 10 percent of their peer group.[112]

"Even one distinguishing strength nearly doubles your chances of being inspiring—and the more distinguishing strengths you have, the more inspirational you can be," they wrote in *How Leaders Inspire*. "No combination of strengths is statistically more powerful than any other. Inspirational leaders come in many varieties."

If you are in the workplace, this has a significant business impact: A study of nearly fifty thousand leaders by Harvard Business School found that "the ability to inspire creates the highest levels of employee engagement and commitment." This leads to 21 percent greater profitability, a 41 percent reduction in absenteeism, and 59 percent less turnover.[113]

Interestingly, we are not always the best judges of whether we are inspiring. Of all the social leadership skills we have explored, this one can be the hardest to self-assess. In some cases, this may be due to a leader's humility or lack of confidence; in others, it may be a lack of self-awareness. But while many leaders aspire to be inspirational, they often aren't convinced they actually are.

One common reason for this is that many have preconceived—and somewhat narrow—ideas about what being an inspiring leader means. When I talk to people about this, I hear comments like "I can't be inspiring—I don't have that kind of 'extroverted personality,'" "I don't like standing up in front of a crowd," or "I am not senior enough."

In this chapter, we'll explore a broad definition of *inspiration* that focuses on motivating others to take action and encouraging people to work together in support of something greater than themselves. We'll look at ways you can use storytelling to foster a sense of inspiration. And we'll explore how you can inspire others by giving back.

Inspiring through Words and Deeds

Reflection: Whom do you know who really lives their purpose? What impact does this have on you and others they interact with?

If you think back to the work we did in chapter 2, you'll remember that you can get clarity on your reason to be through reflection on your values, strengths, and passions. This process of discovery around your purpose is step one. Living and leading in alignment with it is step two. To lead by example, we have to go beyond self-awareness and take action. It is by sharing our purpose and our passions—through our words and our deeds—that we truly inspire others.

In August 1963, American civil rights activist Martin Luther King Jr. stood on the steps of the Lincoln Memorial in Washington, DC, and called for an end to racism in the United States. While he certainly wasn't the first—or the last—activist supporting this sentiment, his stirring address, later known as the "I Have a Dream" speech, became a defining moment in the civil rights movement and is one of the most iconic speeches in American history.

According to historian Taylor Branch, the dream imagery was not included in the prepared text King shared with the press ahead of the event. Instead, he added these words on the spot, prompted by a cry from supporter and friend Mahalia Jackson, who shouted out to Dr. King, "Tell them about the dream, Martin!"[114] With this encouragement, Dr. King shared his personal dreams of freedom and equality. This part of the speech went on to become its most famous and quotable part.

Dr. King's speech is often cited as an example of powerful, inspiring storytelling, largely due to its conviction and authenticity. This real-time sharing from the heart amplified his message. But Dr. King didn't stop there—he not only spoke with true passion; he aligned all of his work to this same purpose.

At Be Leadership, we work with hundreds of social entrepreneurs and charity founders who similarly lead by example. Many of these leaders work in the areas they do because of personal life experience. I have met social leaders who were child refugees and have gone on to create organizations that give immigrants a stronger start at a new life. I have worked with inspiring individuals who have faced illness, hardship, or loss and have used their experiences to ensure others in the same situations get better support. Equally, I have met leaders who had early opportunities and advantages and want to give others a similar chance. These leaders bring to their work a strong sense of purpose and passion to make a change, and this shines through in every interaction with them.

Several of these leaders have graciously granted me permission to present the stories they shared at Be Leadership workshops. All of these leaders are inspiring individuals committed to making a difference.

Take, for example, Michelle King, who founded Little Miracles, a UK charity that provides hope, joy, and adventure to families with children who have disabilities and life-limiting conditions. King started Little Miracles in 2010 after the birth of her son, Oliver, who spent the first four years of his life in the hospital and underwent 152 operations. She speaks with conviction and from personal experience and has taken this passion into the running of her organization.

"I want to make sure no one feels the isolation and disempowerment we felt during the early years of our son's life," King said. Little Miracles currently supports more than fifteen thousand children and their families across fourteen locations in the UK. "There are over a million severely disabled children in the UK, and I want to make sure none of them goes through what we did."

Bayile Adeoti is another powerful example. When I met her, she told me a story about a woman named Aurah. Adeoti said that Aurah was born to be an entrepreneur. She started selling samosas in a local bar for pocket money when she was twelve years old. By the time she left secondary school at eighteen, she was supplying them to eight bars in her local area. Aurah went on to college and later got married. When her marriage failed, Aurah was left with a low income and two children to look after. She sold some of her belongings to support her family and found extra jobs to help them make ends meet.

When Adeoti's social enterprise, Dechomai, launched courses to help Black and minority women start and upscale their businesses, Adeoti said that Aurah signed up immediately. "This surprised me because Aurah was my role model," Adeoti said. "Aurah was the first entrepreneur I ever knew. She was also my mother."

Like King at Little Miracles, Adeoti built on this early influence and experience and has created a business that continues to give back. Under Adeoti's leadership, Dechomai has gone on to support more than 650 entrepreneurs.

Both King and Adeoti are living in alignment with their reason to be. Their passion and commitment are visible in the work they do every day. But they also are able to inspire others because of their ability to tell meaningful stories.

Reflection: Think about stories from your childhood. Maybe these were read or told to you, or you read them yourself. What made them compelling?

Microsoft executive Jean-Philippe Courtois said being inspiring is one of the key leadership requirements of today. He said inspiring leaders—including the social entrepreneurs he works with—are like King and Adeoti. They are doing impactful work, and they are skilled at talking about the *why*. "It's not about creating a world of fantasies and dreams," he said. "It's really creating strong storytelling."[115]

I agree with Courtois that using storytelling to bring things to life for people is a large part of the inspiring skillset. From my experience, even when leaders are clear on their reason to be, they can't necessarily tell a compelling story about it. Inspiring leaders use a range of

If you are able to articulate your purpose and you live in alignment with it, you are more likely to inspire and serve as a role model for others.

storytelling techniques and styles to provide a powerful vision of the future. Spending time expressing our passions helps us feel happier and more fulfilled, and sharing our love for them can be inspiring. This is key to leading by example: If you are able to articulate your purpose and you live in alignment with it, you are more likely to inspire and serve as a role model for others.

EXERCISE

Telling Your Story

You have drafted a purpose statement, and hopefully you are making decisions that help you live in alignment with it. But how effective are you at sharing it with others? Can you inspire people through your story? Reflect on the following questions to consider key dimensions of bringing your purpose to life:

1 *Who is your audience?*—The form your story takes may change depending on the listener. Consider whom you are sharing with, what context they have or need, and how they will be engaging with your story. Maybe you will share with people you work with, or your entire organization. Perhaps you want to share something online. Think about what will interest your audience and what they need for your story to resonate.

2 *What are your key messages?*—What are you trying to achieve through your communication? What do you want people to remember? It's important that you really home in on what's essential. Most listeners can't retain more than three key ideas.

3 *How much time should you take?*—Most people take longer than they need to communicate. While estimates vary, sources say that most audiences have an attention span of no more than ten minutes.[116] Be as concise and engaging as possible.

4 *How can you increase engagement?*—To inspire, we not only need to be comfortable sharing our story, but we need people to hear it. You can increase engagement around

your reason to be by using emotion, personal examples, and questions—all techniques I have discussed elsewhere in this book. Think about what techniques would suit you. How can you bring your story to life? What are your calls to action?

The Four Power Stances

While it's somewhat counterintuitive, one of the other ways we can inspire others as leaders is to be giving of our power. There are many ways to define power, but our first reaction to this word is often negative. We don't have to think too hard to bring to mind leaders who use their power for domination or control. All too often, in both the political and corporate realms, leaders hold on to power and create a culture of fear.

Reflection: What are your beliefs around power?

These leaders use an expression of power called *power over*. When you lead from a power-over stance, you use force or coercion to maintain your position of authority. When using this type of power, you are controlling others through intimidation. While we see this form of power played out across society, it's not the only option. In fact, there are three alternative expressions of power, or power stances, that we can draw on, all of which involve a form of giving and inspiration: *power to*, *power with*, and *power within*.[117] Let's take a look at each.

Power To

In the accountability ladder I shared in chapter 7, we are in a powerless position when we act as victims, and we gain power as we move up the ladder's rungs. One of the ways to appropriately use the power we gain is empowering others, which is defined formally as "giving authority or power to someone to do something."[118] Empowerment moves us further up the accountability ladder and allows us to be more effective.

In our power framework, this expansive, enabling behavior is called *power to*, in which we give agency to others and believe every individual can make a difference. This is a form of power you'll be familiar with if you're in a management role as it is closely connected to delegation, or the giving of authority that you have been granted. If you do this well, you recognize and leverage the potential and gifts that other people have and that they can bring to a situation.

During the summer of 2020, we had an intern at Be Leadership named Katie Kotler. She went on to Duke University and became part of student government, working on projects to improve students' academic and life experience. During her time on these projects, she learned important lessons about power. "I had a perception that to be a leader you had to be the one at the front—the one taking the wheel and acting. One time when I wanted to take charge of a project, I realized that while I was excited and passionate about it, I didn't have enough expertise. So I attempted to shift my perspective."[119]

This shift in perspective is what empowerment is all about. Kotler added, "You don't have to head the charge to be a leader. You can delegate that to those who are more experienced with those relationships. Recognizing the value that came from diversity of thought and creativity of others allowed me to step back and let others lead."

Power With

Power with is when you use the power of everyone together to make a larger impact. When operating from power with, you share the influence that you're given with those around you. Instead of a top-down approach, you collaborate with others and draw on the diversity of the people you're working with to make a bigger impact together. This form of power is closely connected to the social leadership skills of curiosity, flexibility, transparency, and collaboration.

In our Be Leadership workshops, we often use a team problem-solving approach called *action learning*.[120] Action learning is a great example of using the power-with stance. Leaders who participate in this process leverage the diversity of the group to increase their impact and get stronger outcomes.

Action learning brings together a set of four to eight people who use questions to solve real problems while developing leadership skills. It strikes a balance between learning and getting to action. The success of the process lies in the diverse perspectives of the group—instead of relying on subject matter expertise and tossing around solutions, team members use questions and draw upon their unique perspectives and experiences to find new, breakthrough ideas.

You don't have to use action learning to use power with. You have opportunities in your leadership to collaborate with others and share power in a similar way. Simply increasing the number of questions you ask and bringing a diverse set of people into your decision-making will increase your impact.

Power Within

Finally, there is *power within*. This power stance offers clarity and understanding around a situation you are in, and importantly, a realization that you can do something about it. Once you have this awareness, it leads to higher levels of self-worth and dignity.

You may be familiar with the term *agency*—if we have a sense of agency, we can see a way to have some control over actions and their consequences. This is a powerful concept. Agency is equivalent to a path through a challenging situation, or a feeling that we are in charge and can act.[121] We need agency to feel a sense of hope. Agency is an important component of power within.

As a starting place for power within, I would encourage you to think back to your work on values and purpose. When you understand and can articulate your reason to be, you can draw upon power within—both individually and collectively. This form of power gives us the strength and ability to challenge assumptions and imagine—and even create—a better future.

Power Is Not a Finite Resource

One of the biggest differences between power over and the other three types is our belief around whether it is a finite resource. When we work from a position of power with, power to, or power within, we believe that when we let some of our power go, we're not going to run out. Instead, it can actually expand when it's given away. These three

Power over	**Power to**
Using control, force, or coercion to maintain power. Motivation is typically through fear. Power over benefits the minority and oppresses the majority.	Empowering and giving authority to others. Each individual has the power to make a difference. Power to acknowledges individuals' unique potential.

Power with	**Power within**
Shared power that grows out of collaboration and respect for differences. Power with multiplies individual talents and resources to make a larger impact.	Foundation of self-worth. Power within gives individuals agency to challenge assumptions and look for new ways to achieve the common good.

forms of expansive power also look to reduce fear and uncertainty through transparency and the better sharing of information. All of this inspires and motivates people to come together using the connection skills that I focus on throughout this book.

As opposed to those who use power over, leaders who work from a position of power to, with, and within do the following:

- Believe that power becomes infinite and expands when shared with others
- Leverage connection and empathy to unite and stabilize
- Offer transparency to reduce fear and uncertainty
- Create flexible learning cultures, where getting it right is more important than being right
- Move away from shame and blame toward accountability and meaningful change
- Frame leadership as a responsibility to be in service of others rather than served by others
- Lead by example

I'd love to say that during my time as a leader, I have used only the expansive forms of power, but that would not be true. I can think of times when, even now, I take the power I am granted and hold on to it for dear life. And then, inadvertently, I lead others around me from a position of domination and fear. I'm embarrassed to admit that. Reflecting on it now, it's obvious that these are the moments when I am least effective as a leader.

What these situations have in common is that they are all times when I am feeling vulnerable or insecure. Either I feel out of my depth from a skills perspective, or I feel unsure of my level of sponsorship. Sometimes I feel things are getting out of control. Giving power away feels risky—I need to hold on to what I have.

When we work from a position of power with, power to, or power within, we believe that when we let some of our power go, we're not going to run out.

In these situations, if I shared my power instead of holding tight, I would scale my effectiveness and increase my leadership impact.

I'm sure you can relate to this. We all have times where we feel less confident and face vulnerability. Perhaps it's a time of crisis or things have gone off track. Maybe we have a tight deadline, and we feel our reputation is at risk. Our natural inclination is to take back control and be more directive. How can we do this without leading from a position of fear?

The answer is to draw on the other social leadership skills. When we provide enough context for our decision-making and create enough connection with people, we can lead from power with or power to, even if we're directive in our style.

What's Your Power Stance?

When you are faced with a situation where you are questioning your use of power, stop and run through this checklist of reflections before moving forward:

- What type of power are you using right now?

- How comfortable would you feel sharing your power?

What would be the impact of this, positive and negative?

- What are you afraid of that might be causing you to hold on to power?

- What would the consequences be of operating from a different power stance?

- How can you take back power without using power over?

- What power do you have to give today?

What Else Do We Have to Give?

I have spent a lot of time covering power, but this is only one of many gifts we have to give as leaders. Giving is also inspiring in many other forms. Often, in fact, it is provided in the form of service. Inspiring individuals lead by example—acting as good role models who show people what's possible by infusing energy and passion into their behaviors and actions. When we lead in this way, we give back—we contribute to something larger than ourselves through service leadership.

During his long Microsoft career, Jean-Philippe Courtois has moved closer and closer to his personal purpose, which centers on giving back and service leadership. He focuses on this in his day job, where he helps facilitate partnerships between Microsoft customers and countries to use technology for positive impact. But in his free time, he also helps to run a social enterprise he and his family founded in 2015 called Live for Good, which supports young social entrepreneurs in France, and he hosts a podcast called *Positive Leadership* that includes a segment on a leader's role in the world. Courtois sees giving as an essential skill for leaders today: "All leaders should think about who they are working in service of. This

> *Inspiring individuals lead by example—acting as good role models who show people what's possible by infusing energy and passion into their behaviors and actions.*

isn't just about giving to the people you're working with, or the people who are working for you, but it's also giving back to the world."[122]

As leaders, we all have the opportunity like Courtois to become more inspiring to others by shifting to a giving mindset. This includes considering how you might contribute to the broader community and make a positive difference. Giving leaders know when to ask for help, seeking out appropriate guidance and support. Giving can include reaching out, communicating with others, or showing appreciation. It is in this way that being inspiring and giving relate to one another. We are most inspiring when we are generous with our time, energy, knowledge, skills, and feedback.

In my work, I've had the opportunity to get to know hundreds of giving leaders who lead by example. These inspiring individuals hold roles that range from interns to community volunteers, c-suite executives to social entrepreneurs. Being giving isn't dependent on a specific position or title. Instead, it's a mindset.

Small Acts of Kindness

Sometimes we can get overwhelmed by thinking we have to do big things to be a giver. But actually, the most impactful gifts often aren't grand gestures but instead are those that seem small in the giving. Like courage, generosity is built in the minutiae—the decisions you make day to day.

Adam Rifkin, film director, producer, actor, and screenwriter, looks for ways to do what he calls "five-minute favors": small but meaningful gestures that matter. This inspired organizational psychologist and author Adam Grant, who said Rifkin told him, "You don't have to be Mother Teresa or Gandhi to be a giver. You just have to find small ways to add large value to other people's lives."[123]

> *We are most inspiring when we are generous with our time, energy, knowledge, skills, and feedback.*

Five-Minute Favors

Commit now to developing one aspect of giving. By investing just five minutes of your time, you can give people opportunity, power, credit, feedback, acknowledgment, encouragement, or love.

While the list of ways you could give back is endless, here are a few examples of small acts that make a large difference. Choose one every week and do it. You might consider adding an appointment to your calendar or recurring item in your to-do list to prompt you.

- *Make an introduction*—Connect two people who might benefit from knowing each other.

- *Share your knowledge and gifts*—Be generous with your wisdom and experience so others can learn from you.

- *Show people you care*—Choose words and actions that show those around you that you consider their work and life significant.

- *Give feedback*—Provide credit and praise to others for work well done and direct and constructive feedback to help support development.

- *Stand up for people*—Give support and assistance when people need it, individually or collectively.

- *Provide appreciation*—Recognize someone whose work has gone unnoticed.

- *Celebrate success*—Take time to acknowledge achievements and celebrate successes of both individuals and teams before moving on to new projects.

CEO Vlada Bortnik incorporates some of these small acts of giving into the workweek at Marco Polo. Every Wednesday, she dedicates their company-wide Zoom meeting to appreciation. Employees are invited to type colleagues' names into the chat box and then they are called on to share praise out loud. Bortnik said that in the early days, she had to encourage people to participate, but now this form of giving is an embedded part of the culture: "Inevitably I'll have to type 'let's stop here' because so many names are shared," she said.[124]

Rifkin has learned through experience that giving through these "favors" can be impactful for those on the receiving end, even if the gifts only take five minutes: "Time is the currency that no one can really buy more of," Rifkin noted.[125] "If you're paying with your time rather than paying with cash, it's more meaningful. Especially when you're busy."

And while this practice shouldn't be about keeping score, over time the benefit can come back to you: research has shown that giving lowers your blood pressure, reduces your stress levels, and increases longevity.[126]

Take Action

You are inspiring, even if you don't see it. There are so many ways to give back, and making these into simple habits will help you be a more effective leader. In addition to the five-minute favors we explored earlier, here are some simple steps you can take:

1 *Delegate more*—Most of us want things done a certain way, which means giving up power or control is difficult. Remember that delegating worthwhile work is a gift of growth and development for someone else.

2 *Give opportunity*—Whom do you know who needs a second chance? How can you create the right circumstances for them to succeed? Consider what opportunities you can create for someone who is deserving but not in a position to be noticed. Give others a chance to achieve their goals.

3 *Practice receiving*—To produce a culture of giving and inspire those around you, role model receiving feedback well. Respond with a simple "Thank you, I really appreciate that."

4 *Assume positive intent*—In any given interaction, start by assuming the other person is genuinely working toward a positive outcome and means well. Notice how that starting point affects both your communication and the experience you have with the other person.

5 *Stop keeping score*—Organizational psychologist Adam Grant frequently talks about three styles of leaders: givers, takers, and matchers.[127] Matchers usually give, expecting something in return. They operate on the principle of fairness and reciprocity. Does that describe you? If so, experiment with letting this mindset go and focus on the positive feeling you get by being generous.

6 *Get your hands dirty*—Inspire those around you by spending a day working alongside your team, taking on roles usually done by others. Learn what they are doing to be

more effective, and ask questions about what they enjoy and where they struggle. This is a great way to build trust while continuing to develop your skills.

Making even small changes can help you lead by example. Remember, we all have the power within ourselves to be role models and inspire others to action. Getting clear on your passions and purpose will give you a head start on our final chapter, where we'll discuss branding and impact.

Chapter 9

Building Your Leadership Brand

Because we all have an impact

If you asked those around you to describe your leadership, what words would they use?

"Identity is cause; brand is effect, and the strength of the former influences the strength of the latter."

—Larry Ackerman, author of *The Identity Code*

R ecently, I awoke thinking about branding, so I was acutely aware of the prevalence of logos and brand identification as I put on my running clothes. My shirt, shoes, running cap, and even my socks had visible signs of the companies that make them. What made me choose one pair of shoes over another? What made me pick the running jacket I wore to stay dry in the rain? I continued this observation throughout my day: How did I select the computer I am typing on, the jewelry I wear, and the car that I drive?

As consumers, we are influenced by a company's brand and often, consciously or unconsciously, choose products because of what that company represents. Big corporations focus intently on their branding and what's called their "brand value," which refers to the worth of a brand to us as consumers. Brand value can be measured by how often people choose one brand over its alternatives. It also can be measured in financial terms: The financial worth of a brand is calculated based on current and future sales as well as potential for future growth. Many household names have a brand value worth billions of dollars.

Sometimes a brand identity has an overwhelmingly positive impact on public perception. Most often, in these cases, it's because the actions of the organization and its leadership are consistent with its words. Take, for example, the case of Patagonia, an American-headquartered company that designs and manufactures clothing and gear for outdoor sports. Its mission is to be "in business to save our home planet," and the company operates in close alignment with this in every decision it takes. Because this commitment to the planet was so core to the company's ethos from its foundation in the 1970s, its founder, Yvon Chouinard, was highly lauded in 2022 when he decided to restructure the company so all of its profits would help fight the climate crisis.[128]

In an unconventional move, Chouinard donated 2 percent of all stock and all decision-making to a trust, then transferred the remaining 98 percent of the company's stock to a nonprofit called the Holdfast Collective, which was committed to supporting the environment. At the time, he told the press, "Instead of going public, you could say we're going purpose."[129]

Companies like Patagonia gain a powerful competitive advantage when people see them as distinctive, consistent, and authentic. When consumers or clients see companies as aligned with their own personal values, it increases brand loyalty, and they will go out of their way to select that brand over the other options. They will, in fact, go so far as to pay more for that brand. But if a company's reputation is eroded by lack of brand consistency or perceived inauthenticity, they will avoid a brand at all costs.

What Is Leadership Branding?

Branding clearly has an impact on our purchasing decisions (and our wallet), but if we look beyond our role as a consumer, why does it matter?

Just like a company, each of us has a brand. Among our community of family and friends, we have a reputation—a *personal brand* that we hope reflects our priorities, the values we stand for, the offerings or promises we consistently deliver, and how we go about delivering them. If we consider that our purpose is an overarching sense of what matters, or our reason to be, our personal brand is how we bring this to life in our interactions. It dictates how interested people are in spending time with us, how they feel when they leave any interaction we have, and how likely they are to go above and beyond to help us when we are in need.

> *If we consider that our purpose is an overarching sense of what matters, or our reason to be, our personal brand is how we bring this to life in our interactions.*

Our personal brand needs to have real conviction if it's going to have an impact. In other words, you must really, really believe in it. And it needs to be consistent. You need to live and breathe your brand for it to be credible.

At work or in other similar social contexts, your personal brand extends to your *leadership brand*. This is how you interact with others to produce results. You can look at your leadership brand as who you are and what you want to be known for as a leader.

If we look back at corporate branding and how to measure brand value, we find a range of factors, including the following:

- *Awareness*—How many people have heard of your brand?

- *Image*—What are others' perceptions of your brand?

- *Understanding*—How well do consumers truly understand what your brand offers?

- *Consideration*—What do consumers consider when choosing your brand over the competition?

- *Loyalty*—How willing are customers to stay with you over the competition?

All of these same considerations can be taken at an individual level, as we'll explore in the following exercise, and when you look at these together, it can help you think about the reputation you have today and how closely aligned this is to the leadership brand you wish to create.

What Is Your Brand?

Take a look at the five factors that help measure brand value and apply them to yourself. Spend time honestly answering the following questions and see where you are with your leadership brand—and where you want to be:

- *Awareness*—How visible are you?

- *Image*—What is your leadership reputation? How do people know you as a leader?

- *Understanding*—How clearly do people recognize your values, passions, and strengths?

- *Consideration*—What would people take into account when deciding whether to collaborate or partner with you?

- *Loyalty*—How willing are people to stay by your side?

Why Brand Matters

The concept of branding dates back thousands of years. In their most basic form, brands are symbols that depict ownership and indicate origin. As such, the earliest use of the word centered on farmers who branded their cattle to identify them from the livestock that belonged to their neighbors, and ancient artisans who used symbols and engravings to distinguish their work from that of others.

Leadership brand is similar—it's what you are known for, and what sets you apart. It is the impression that you leave people with after they spend time with you. As businessperson and author Robert Kiyosaki said it, "If you are not a brand, you are a commodity."[130] While purpose is your reason to be across your whole existence or what really matters to you in life, your leadership brand is the value you offer, or at an aspirational level, it's *your purpose brought to life in your work*.

> *While purpose is your reason to be across your whole existence or what really matters to you in life, your leadership brand is the value you offer, or at an aspirational level, it's your purpose brought to life in your work.*

As you know by now, social leadership is about skills, perspectives, and self-awareness. So a lot of our work as leaders starts with recognizing and acknowledging our current reputation and how closely aligned this is with where we want to be. We then can decide what type of promise we want to make as a leader.

While the sum of your previous interactions and experiences with other people may be in the past, the personal leadership brand you aspire to should guide you into the future. It's about the decisions you make each day and who you want to be—the legacy that you're leaving through what you do and who you are.

As with your purpose, there is a benefit to getting to a place where you can express your leadership brand with confidence. Here are some concrete reasons why clarifying your leadership brand really makes a difference:

1 *Your leadership brand differentiates you from others.*
When you have a clear and identifiable leadership brand, other people recognize your unique contributions. If, for example, your strengths are in collaborating, being resourceful, or asking courageous questions, other people associate these skills with you and your leadership. This is beneficial to you and the broader team or organization. It means that you will be brought into positions and projects where those talents are valued, and you will be given more opportunity to do the type of work you really enjoy.

2 *You can use your brand to guide your decision-making.*
Once you have a leadership brand statement that is real and true for you (see the next exercise), you can use this as a guide to inspire your decision-making on a daily basis. Like your purpose, your leadership brand can and should be forward looking and aspirational: none of us live in alignment with our purpose or our brand all the time, but when we are able to express it with conviction, it will inspire us to make better choices.

3 *Your leadership brand can support your career aspirations.*
No matter what goals you have for your career, clarity on your leadership brand can help you focus in on the options that are best aligned to your strengths, passions, and values. Not only will a clear brand statement help you answer questions about your longer-term aspirations during interviews and career conversations, but precision around this will ensure you make better choices around where to apply and what roles to target.

4 *Your leadership brand can help you expand your impact.*
To be an effective social leader, it's important to think not only about what you do but how you do it. Your leadership brand should be represented in what you achieve and also how you engage with others. It's through both of these dimensions—the how and the what—that you can enhance your leadership impact. Do you collaborate well

The way you engage in the social process of leadership helps you to widen and deepen your impact, which has a lasting impression on others.

with others? Do you give clear and generous feedback? Do you maintain a beginner's mindset and keep yourself open to new input? The way you engage in the social process of leadership helps you to widen and deepen your impact, which has a lasting impression on others.

Bringing Your Leadership Brand to Life

In chapter 2, I introduced a way of thinking about purpose that was adapted from work by David Mead, Peter Docker, and Simon Sinek in *Find Your Why*.[131] This purpose statement has a simple structure:

My purpose is to _____

so that _____.

Take a minute to find the purpose statement you created, because we're going to expand on it.

In creating this purpose statement, I encouraged you to consider your values, passions, and strengths, as these elements can help you get to the heart of your reason to be. As an example, my personal purpose statement is *to spark passion in others so together we can create a better world*. This inspires me in my work as well as my broader life. When I partner with clients to develop leaders and increase their impact, I can see this purpose in action. And it also guides what I do outside work, with my parenting and community volunteering as well as how I choose to spend my time.

Within this purpose statement, we consider both the contribution we hope to make in the world and the impact it has, but we can extend this to our leadership brand by considering *how* it comes to life when we are interacting with others.

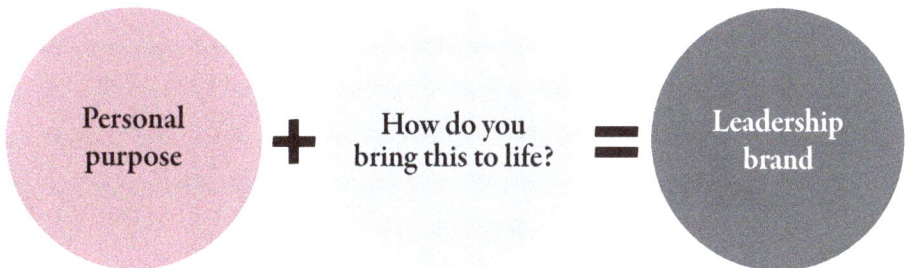

Personal purpose **+** **How do you bring this to life?** **=** **Leadership brand**

At a statement level, it looks like this:

As a leader, I (contribution) by (how) so that (impact).

In my own purpose statement, I can consider questions like: What can I do in my work to spark passion in others? How can we create a positive impact through the work we do together? This helps me to articulate the difference between my purpose and my leadership brand statement, which becomes: *As a leader, I spark passion in others by role modeling, mentoring, and coaching, so together we can create a better world.*

What is new in this version is the *how*—our purpose encapsulates our whole life, and people can see it within our leadership through the actions we take and how we behave.

EXERCISE

Leadership Brand Statement

To help you reflect on this step of shifting from your purpose statement to your leadership brand, consider these questions:

- How do you define your purpose?

- What are you known for as a leader today?

- When are you most happy in the organizations you are part of?

- What is the impact that you want to have on the world?

- How is your purpose brought to life in your work?

- What could you do to increase your leadership impact?

Having reflected on these questions, take some time to write your leadership brand statement down. Read it out loud. Try sharing it with some people you trust, and have them ask you questions about it. It is often through this process of sharing that your ideas crystallize, and you gain confidence around what it means for you.

Being Comfortable with the Expansive

Sometimes in our leadership programs we get to the point where people are writing down their leadership brands, and they express concern that their statements feel too aspirational or expansive. In one of my programs, I had a leader who said he came to the conclusion that the impact he wanted to have was improving the world, but as he hadn't "won a Nobel Prize," he struggled to take ownership of a purpose that had this broad an ambition. Another felt their brand would sound too idealistic and therefore wouldn't come across as authentic. One leader shared a powerful leadership brand statement and then said, "Surely everyone would say they want to achieve this? Couldn't this apply to anyone?"

Remember, if honestly and authentically crafted, your leadership brand is yours. You won't always live up to it, but it represents what you want to become and how you wish to lead. Articulating and managing your brand is a powerful way to be authentic and a true agent for yourself. The closer you get to your real purpose and leadership brand statement, and the more times you repeat it, the more comfortable you will feel articulating it to others.

Reflection: What kind of legacy do you want to leave?

Your brand and purpose are synonymous with the reputation you aspire to. By thinking strategically about this, you are taking control of this reputation and ensuring it reflects who you really are. While it may seem that your leadership brand sounds like a horoscope that could be true for anyone, there are as many unique brand statements as there are leaders.

Discovering what you want your leadership brand to be focuses your actions. It helps you clarify what you should be doing as well as what you should stop doing. It only makes sense for people to understand how they are viewed by others and if that doesn't match their wishes, to take steps to close the gap and ensure their abilities, values, and passions are truly understood.

Take Action

I wrote this book because *every one of us has an impact*. That impact can be positive, or it can be negative; it can be narrow, or it can be world changing. We impact those around us, and by extension our families, organizations, and communities. We might not even be aware of it in the moment, but the impressions we make can last a lifetime. We are making an impact in the way we choose to live, the way we choose to work, and the way we choose to lead.

Your leadership brand, when well defined and articulated, can help guide your decisions and support a life that is happier and more balanced. When you decide—and proactively take steps—to develop your social leadership skills and lead in alignment with your purpose, it makes a difference. Here are specific actions you can take to support the work you have done in this chapter:

1 *Find two words*—It can be helpful to identify a short phrase that you feel really sums up your brand's essence. If you were to use no more than two words to represent your leadership brand, what would they be?

2 *Share with your trusted circle*—Select some people you really trust, and share your purpose and leadership brand with them. Get some feedback. Practice saying your purpose out loud. It becomes more natural and easier with time. If it doesn't feel quite right, refine it and try again.

3 *Update your profile*—When you feel comfortable that your brand really represents you and your leadership aspirations, incorporate it into your LinkedIn profile, your résumé or CV, or other public bios.

4 *Hold a personal Think Week*—In chapter 7, I mentioned that I hold an annual Think Week where I step away from my client work at Be Leadership and think strategically about the company's objectives. While I appreciate it's an investment and not necessarily possible to take a vacation for this, you can still designate a week every year as your personal Think Week. Find time that week to reflect on your purpose, learning goals, and leadership brand.

Consider where you are focused and how you are leading, and reflect on the shifts you could make to create more alignment.

What we've covered throughout this book has led to this: a deeper understanding of your reason to be; an aspirational purpose statement and leadership brand that incorporate your values, passions, and strengths; and tools that support you in all aspects of your personal and professional life. Now it's your turn. What kind of leader are you going to be today? What about tomorrow?

This is a process that can and should be ongoing. In the words of Brother David Steindl-Rast, author, scholar, and Benedictine monk, "Being human means becoming what we are. If you stopped becoming, you would cease to be. Yet in the process of becoming, you cease to be what you were."[32] Each day you have an opportunity to start again and to think about how you invest your time and how you respond to situations. What is within your control? What is your mindset? How are you using your leadership skills? And what perspectives are you bringing to your decisions?

I encourage you to find your personal cause—your reason to be, your purpose—and continually reflect on how you are leading. Why? Because it makes a difference. Because you have an impact. And because you are never done becoming the leader you could be.

Glossary of Skills

ACCOUNTABLE   Accountable leaders hold themselves and others to a high standard. Being accountable is more than just being responsible for something—it's also being answerable for your actions. Accountability is about clearly sharing ownership and delegating where appropriate while delivering on what's been promised. Highly accountable leaders use resources around them well. They engage and collaborate effectively with others to reach objectives. They manage expectations well so others can trust their word. At their core, accountable leaders are reliable and have high integrity.

AUTHENTIC   Authenticity is about alignment between our values and our actions. Authentic leaders share their "true selves" with those around them. On a practical level, this means being honest and open about strengths and weaknesses, admitting mistakes, and expressing a certain degree of vulnerability. We regard leaders as authentic when their conduct is in congruence with what they truly believe. To develop authenticity, consider the message you are sending about yourself through your daily interactions. Choose your words and behaviors thoughtfully and in alignment with who you are as a person.

COLLABORATIVE   In too many organizations, leaders hold on to control and communicate from the top down. This can lead to unempowered teams and slower decision-making. Collaborative leaders, in contrast, form rich connections and engage in two-way dialogue. They proactively reach out to people to get their input, invest time in building authentic relationships, and incorporate the input they hear. They create environments that allow for real engagement. Collaboration is a fundamental social leadership behavior: through real collaboration, teams and organizations can build the trust required to operate effectively.

COURAGEOUS   To be successful, modern organizations need courageous leaders. Courage in the workplace takes many forms: Sometimes it's the willingness to speak up and share your views, even when it's difficult. Sometimes it's challenging the status quo. Other times it means trying a new approach or making a decision that is unpopular. Being a courageous leader requires taking bold but appropriate risks, being willing to fail, and then learning from that failure to create new success. Taking these steps can be scary, but through courageous behavior, leaders build trust within their organizations and foster innovation.

CURIOUS   Curious leaders are always learning. They don't focus on having all the answers, but instead explore ideas with an open mind. They look for novel solutions to old problems, seek out additional perspectives, and identify new ways to think and behave. Curious leaders ask a lot of open questions, which help to identify new avenues for exploration and can lead to breakthrough ideas. These open, curious questions help to ensure a problem is looked at from all angles before jumping to a solution. To develop curiosity, reflect on how many open questions you ask and how actively you listen.

FLEXIBLE   In today's workplace, we need flexible leaders who are agile, responsive to change, and willing to learn. Flexible leaders are open to new input when making a decision, and able to change their minds or compromise based on new data. They seek out and appreciate diverse points of view. Leaders with a flexible, or growth, mindset are open to the belief that they learn through action. Whether they succeed or fail, flexible leaders can reflect on their experiences and apply their learning to their work for better future results. In flexible leadership, resilience and hard work lead to better outcomes.

GIVING   Givers focus on what others need and endeavor to be generous with their time, energy, knowledge, skills, and feedback. They also know when to ask for help, seeking out appropriate guidance and support. As leaders, we have an opportunity to shift our mindset to one that is more oriented toward giving. Giving relates closely to service leadership, where one considers how they might contribute to the broader community and make a positive difference. By developing as a giver, you create a trusting climate where everyone feels they can contribute, which can increase innovation.

INCLUSIVE   Inclusive leaders are committed to a true exploration of diverse views and perspectives. They surround themselves with people who are different from them and seek out ideas that may challenge those they hold. They are willing to unlearn and relearn. Inclusive leaders are aware of the biases and weaknesses they may have and engage in ongoing reflection about this. On a practical level, inclusive leaders recognize and value the uniqueness of each individual while accepting each person fully. To develop inclusive leadership, you must step outside your comfort zone and look at situations from new angles.

INSPIRING   Inspiring leaders motivate others to take action, encouraging people to work together in the service of something greater than themselves. They offer a clear sense of direction and purpose, and they are skilled at providing a compelling vision of the future. Part of being inspirational involves storytelling—while the stories can take many forms, inspiring leaders bring things to life for people. Often, inspiration is provided in the form of service. Inspiring leaders are frequently good role models who show others what's possible through their own behaviors and actions.

PRESENT   Presence can often be challenging in the modern workplace. Present leaders focus on one thing at a time, avoid distraction, and listen actively. They demonstrate through their body language that they are fully engaged. When we are present as leaders, we ask better, more relevant questions; we are able to build on what's been said more effectively; and we can more appropriately bring emotion into our replies. As a leader, you can develop greater levels of presence by focusing on "now": remove distractions during meetings, turn off unneeded devices, practice appropriate eye contact, and summarize what you've heard.

RESOURCEFUL   As leaders today, we can no longer rely strictly on subject matter expertise. Information is more freely available, and content is more quickly out of date. Resourceful leaders are those who can pull together data from many sources and see patterns and connections, consolidating and then filtering the information to make sense of it in new contexts. While they know when to trust their own judgment, resourceful leaders also know where to go to find solutions. They enjoy experimenting and are skilled in imagining new innovative possibilities.

TRANSPARENT   We live in a world of rapid change. This requires more transparency from our leaders. Transparent leaders reduce threat and uncertainty in their organizations by being as clear as possible with information, sharing what is real and true. They put an emphasis on openness, knowing that this context setting can result in more informed decision-making. Transparent leaders also share ideas in their earlier stages, increasing inclusivity and trust by engaging people and getting input before plans are final. To practice transparency, consider what projects you have underway and who might benefit from a preview. Start sharing.

Group Exercises

W hile most of the exercises earlier in this book are ones you can take on as an individual, you can amplify your impact by involving others. Here are some group exercises you can use to share your skills and learnings around social leadership. You could decide to read the book together as a team and try these exercises as you finish each chapter, or you may decide to use just one or two to support a group's development.

Chapter 1: Social Leadership in Practice

Leadership in Action

Objective: This exercise helps you and your team recognize what the social leadership skills look like in practice and which are most important to you individually and collectively.

Time Required: Minimum 20 minutes

Number of People Needed: 3+

Instructions:

1 In pairs or trios, describe someone you most admire. Why do you admire them? What skills and behaviors do they demonstrate?

2 If working with a larger group, come back together and share examples of the skills and behaviors that surfaced in the smaller group conversations.

3 Discuss both the similarities and differences between leaders who are admired:

- *What social leadership skills do these individuals embody?*
- *What can you learn from this?*

Chapter 2: Exploring Your Reason to Be

The River of Life

Objective: This exercise is designed to help you and your team reflect on your backgrounds and personal journeys. It helps individuals on your team get clarity on their values and strengths, while helping the team as a whole create a higher level of psychological safety and connection.

Time Required: Minimum 1–2 hours

Number of People Needed: 3+

Instructions:

1 While the River of Life is a group exercise, you must first start with some individual reflection. Everyone should have a piece of paper and writing utensils, ideally in multiple colors.

2 Direct your team members to draw a river that represents their life, with birth at the bottom and present moment at the top. On one side, draw tributaries that illustrate moments of pride, triumph, accomplishment, excitement, and joy. On the other side, draw tributaries that illustrate moments of failure, difficulty, worry, grief, and sadness.

3 Ask team members to draw circles near the river to represent people who have influenced their lives. They can draw bridges, rocks, and any other symbols that illustrate the ups and downs of life. Allow at least thirty minutes for this work.

4 Once everyone has finished their river, join up in groups of three to four people, and discuss the stories of your rivers as well as the following questions:

- *What values, commitments, causes, or principles have been most important to you at any given point during your life?*

- *What purposes and goals have shaped the flow of your river throughout your life?*

- How would you relate what you see in your river to the approach you take as a leader?

5 When everyone has had an opportunity to share, come back to the larger group if there is one and discuss your takeaways:

- What patterns or trends do you notice?
- What have you learned from this exercise?

Chapter 3: Leading with Courageous Authenticity

Leading with Courage

Objective: This exercise calls for some self-reflection on times when you have acted with courage or lacked courage in the past, and most importantly, encourages group reflection around how you can go forth with more courageous authenticity in the future.

Time Required: Minimum 30 minutes

Number of People Needed: 3+ but more ideal for medium to large groups

Instructions:

1 Break into groups of three to four people, and discuss the following two scenarios:

- Scenario 1: Think of situations when you took a stand as a leader and made sure everyone followed. What were the circumstances? How did you feel? How do you think others felt? What was the impact of your actions?
- Scenario 2: Think of situations when you didn't take a stand on a particular issue but feel you should have. What were the circumstances? How did you feel during and afterward? How do you think others felt? What was the impact of your inaction?

2 Discuss everyone's individual experiences:

- How were the situations similar?
- How were they different?

- *How could we make different choices to be more coura-geous and authentic in our leadership?*

3 If there are multiple smaller groups, come back together as a larger group and discuss your takeaways.

Chapter 4: Adopting a Beginner's Mindset

Seven Questions

Objective: This exercise helps you develop more awareness around the quality of your questions and whether they are open or closed. It illustrates the power of open questions to encourage reflection, creativity, and expanded perspective.

Time Required: Minimum 30 minutes

Number of People Needed: 3+ but ideal for medium to large groups

Instructions:

1 Create trios, where two of the group members will have a conversation and the third group member will act as an observer.

2 Person 1 describes a current challenge or situation in one to two sentences.

3 Person 2 asks an open question based on this statement.

4 Person 1 answers (only) the question asked.

5 Person 2 asks a new question based on the last response.

6 If a closed question is asked, the observer calls it out and has them start over.

7 Continue until you reach seven questions, then swap roles.

8 Once all groups have finished, as a team, discuss everyone's experiences and thoughts on this exercise:

- *What did you learn from this experience?*
- *How did it make you feel?*
- *How do you think you will bring this exercise to life?*

Chapter 5: Harnessing Diverse Thinking

Diversity Flower

Objective: This activity creates a space for your team to learn more about each other's backgrounds, interests, and perspectives. This deeper understanding helps the team to better appreciate its diversity while finding previously unacknowledged or hidden commonalities.

Time Required: Minimum 30 minutes

Number of People Needed: 8+ and ideal for larger groups

Instructions:

1 Start by dividing teams into groups of four or more participants and provide each group with flip-chart paper and colorful markers.

2 Ask each group to draw a flower that has a large center. The number of flower petals should equal the number of people in that group.

3 Ask participants to identify a trait that they have in common and fill the center of the flower with this word(s). Then each group member will fill a petal with a word(s) describing something that makes them unique.

4 Ask the groups to exchange flowers with other groups and discuss the common and unique traits across the whole team.

Chapter 6: Building Teams That Talk

A Team Agreement

Objective: Creating a team agreement allows your team to collectively identify a set of values, principles, or behaviors that you would like to embody and demonstrate to improve communication and collaboration.

Time Required: Minimum 60 minutes
Number of People Needed: Ideally done with your entire team
Instructions:

1 Review the concept of a team agreement from page 112. As a team, schedule some time to get together as a group to discuss these ideas.

2 Create a set of questions to ask your team to help them think about how they want to work together. Refer to chapter 6 for sample questions to discuss and share with the team, both around mechanics and dynamics.

3 As a group, create a team agreement.

4 Remember to refer back to this agreement frequently with questions for reflection:

- *How well are we following our team agreement?*

- *What are we doing well? What could we do even better?*

- *What is the impact when we follow this agreement? When we don't?*

- *What should we do moving forward?*

Chapter 7: Focusing on Accountability

Stop Playing the Victim

Objective: This exercise helps you practice being more aware of your mindset in times when you feel frustration, inequality, or a lack of control. You can decide how you respond in these difficult situations: as a victim, who focuses on things you cannot influence, or with accountability, focusing on elements within your power.
Time Required: Minimum 45 minutes
Number of People Needed: 6+ but more ideal for larger groups

Instructions:

1 Review the concept of victim mentality from page 131. As a team, schedule some time to get together as a group to discuss these ideas.

2 Create trios and ask half the groups to look at the following scenario with a victim mindset and half with a mindset of accountability.

- *Scenario 1: You're currently leading two projects and have too much work to do to keep both projects on track. You've told each of your teams when you can be available, but they keep scheduling you for meetings outside of your available windows. You feel worn out, frustrated, and like a failure.*

3 In your trios, discuss what your assigned mindset looks like in response to this scenario. Use and write "I" statements in your reflections as a group. A victim-oriented statement might be "Why am I the only one working so hard?" or "I guess I'll just have to do it all." An accountable-oriented statement might be something like "I'm going to delegate some of my responsibilities to other team members when I'm overloaded," or "I need to decide which of these responsibilities is highest priority."

4 Once all groups have completed this first scenario, repeat the same exercise in the same groups, but this time with the opposite mindset—meaning if your group used a victim mindset the first time, switch to accountable for this one, and vice versa.

- *Scenario 2: You're working on a team with someone who drives you crazy. They always interrupt when you are discussing ideas. They also seem to talk about your ideas or the team's ideas as if they were their own.*

5 Repeat the group reflection, continuing to use "I" statements. Examples of the victim mindset in this scenario might be "No one appreciates my work," or "I don't really

matter to this team," whereas an accountable statement could be "I need to have a direct conversation with this person to tell them how this behavior is impacting me."

6 When all the groups have concluded their work on the second scenario, come back together as a large group and share your statements and thoughts:

- *How did this exercise make you feel?*
- *What are your takeaways?*

Chapter 8: Leading by Example

A Gift and an Ask

Objective: This short exercise can be used as an icebreaker to create deeper connection across your team and greater transparency around what each person needs to be effective.
Time Required: 10–15 minutes
Number of People Needed: 3+
Instructions:

1 This exercise can be used in a variety of different ways, whether it be as a check-in before meetings, during team-building activities, or in any other moments when you want to get your team feeling more connected.

2 Gift and Ask is simple. All you need to do is share one "Gift" that you are going to bring to your work, such as a strength or something positive you bring to the table. Then, share one "Ask," something you are asking of others to make the work at hand more effective.

3 Everyone in the group should take turns sharing, and in doing so, create a more clear and productive meeting.

Chapter 9: Building Your Leadership Brand

Purpose in the Workplace

Objective: This exercise is a great conclusion to your reading of *Because* and ties together all the work done thus far on finding and building on your leadership brand within the context of your entire team.
Time Required: Minimum 1 hour
Number of People Needed: Ideally your entire team
Instructions:

1 Have your team members work on creating drafts of their individual purpose statements, using the process described in chapter 2. Then dedicate a time to meet as a team to discuss them.

2 When the team comes together, get into small groups of three to four people, and share your draft statements. Support each other through powerful questions.

3 After everyone has completed this step, come back as a larger group, and discuss the purpose statements and takeaways from your small discussions:

- *How do your individual purposes work together as a collective?*

- *What do all these purpose statements mean for your team as a whole?*

- *How does this align with the purpose of the organization or company?*

- *And most importantly, how will each person bring their purpose to life in their work?*

Recommended Resources

Social Leadership in Practice

Epstein, D. *Range: How Generalists Triumph in a Specialized World*. New York: Riverhead Books, 2019.

Johansen, B. *Leaders Make the Future: Ten New Leadership Skills for an Uncertain World*. San Francisco: Berrett-Koehler, 2012.

Johansen, B. *The New Leadership Literacies: Thriving in a Future of Extreme Disruption and Distributed Everything*. Oakland: Berrett-Koehler, 2017.

Murthy, V. H. *Together: Loneliness, Health and What Happens When We Find Connection*. London: Profile Books, 2021.

Exploring Your Reason to Be

Ackerman, L. *The Identity Code: The 8 Essential Questions for Finding Your Purpose and Place in the World*. New York: Random House, 2005.

Esfahani Smith, E. *The Power of Meaning: The True Route to Happiness*. London: Rider, 2017.

Sinek, S. *Start with Why: How Great Leaders Inspire Everyone to Take Action*. New York: Portfolio Penguin, 2009.

Sinek, S., D. Mead, and P. Docker. *Find Your Why: A Practical Guide for Discovering Purpose for You and Your Team*. New York: Portfolio Penguin, 2017.

Leading with Courageous Authenticity

Brown, B. *Atlas of the Heart: Mapping Meaningful Connection and the Language of Human Experience*. New York: Vermilion, Penguin Random House, 2021.

Brown, B. *Daring Greatly: How the Courage to Be Vulnerable Transforms the Way We Live, Love, Parent and Lead*. New York: Gotham Books, 2012.

Detert, J. *Choosing Courage: The Everyday Guide to Being Brave at Work*. Boston: Harvard Business Review Press, 2021.

Goffee, R., and G. Jones. *Why Should Anyone Be Led by You?: What It Takes to Be an Authentic Leader*. Boston: Harvard Business Review Press, 2019.

Joseph, S. *Authentic: How to Be Yourself and Why It Matters*. London: Piatkus, 2016.

Thacker, K. *The Art of Authenticity*. Hoboken: John Wiley & Sons, 2016.

Adopting a Beginner's Mindset

Berger, W. *A More Beautiful Question: The Power of Inquiry to Spark Breakthrough Ideas*. New York: Bloomsbury USA, 2014.

Dweck, C. S. *Mindset: The New Psychology of Success, How We Can Learn to Fulfill Our Potential*. New York: Random House, 2006.

Garvey Berger, J. *Unlocking Leadership Mindtraps: How to Thrive in Complexity*. Redwood City: Stanford University Press, 2019.

Grant, A. *Think Again: The Power of Knowing What You Don't Know*. London: W. H. Allen, 2021.

Gregersen, H. *Questions Are the Answer: A Breakthrough Approach to Your Most Vexing Problems at Work and in Life*. New York: HarperCollins, 2018.

Leslie, I. *Curious: The Desire to Know and Why Your Future Depends on It*. London: Quercus, 2014.

Marquardt, M. *Leading with Questions: How Leaders Find the Right Solutions by Knowing What to Ask*. San Francisco: Jossey-Bass, 2005.

Marquardt, M., S. Banks, P. Cauwelier, and C. S Ng. *Optimizing the Power of Action Learning: Real-Time Strategies for Developing Leaders, Building Teams and Transforming Organizations*. Boston: Nicholas Brealey, 2018.

Harnessing Diverse Thinking

Brown, B. *Braving the Wilderness*. London: Penguin Random House UK, 2017.

D'Souza, S., and D. Renner. *Not Knowing: The Art of Turning Uncertainty into Opportunity*. New York: LID Publishing USA, 2014.

Frost, S. *The Inclusion Imperative: How Real Inclusion Creates Better Business and Builds Better Societies*. London: Kogan Page, 2014.

Hicks, D. *Leading with Dignity: How to Create a Culture That Brings Out the Best in People*. New Haven: Yale University Press, 2019.

Syed, M. *Rebel Ideas: The Power of Diverse Thinking*. New York: Flatiron Books, 2021.

Zheng, L. *DEI Deconstructed: Your No-Nonsense Guide to Doing the Work and Doing It Right*. Oakland: Berrett-Koehler, 2022.

Building Teams That Talk

Groysberg, B., and M. Slind. *Talk, Inc.: How Trusted Leaders Use Conversation to Power Their Organizations*. Boston: Harvard Business School Publishing, 2012.

Whitehurst, J. *The Open Organization: Igniting Passion and Performance*. Boston: Harvard Review Press, 2015.

Focusing on Accountability

Crabbe, T. *Busy: How to Thrive in a World of Too Much*. London: Piatkus, 2015.

Kofman, F. *Conscious Business: How to Build Value through Values*. Louisville: Sounds True, 2013.

Marturano, J. *Finding the Space to Lead: A Practical Guide to Mindful Leadership*. Berryville: Bloomsbury Press, 2014.

Leading by Example

Esfahani Smith, E. *The Power of Meaning: The True Route to Happiness*. London: Rider, 2017.

Grant, A. *Give and Take: A Revolutionary Approach to Success*. London: Weidenfeld and Nicolson, 2013.

Marturano, J. *Finding the Space to Lead: A Practical Guide to Mindful Leadership*. Berryville: Bloomsbury Press, 2014.

Building Your Leadership Brand

Burnett, B., and D. Evans. *Designing Your Life: How to Build a Well-Lived, Joyful Life*. New York: Alfred A. Knopf, 2016.

Chamberlain, S. *On Purpose: What Are You Really Here to Do?* United Kingdom: Printed by the author, 2020.

Kaputa, C. *You Are a Brand!: In Person and Online, How Smart People Brand Themselves for Business Success*. Boston: Nicholas Brealey, 2012.

Springer, K. *I Am My Brand: How to Build Your Brand without Apology*. New York: Bloomsbury USA, 2020.

Acknowledgments

This is simultaneously the most rewarding section of this book to write and the most difficult. It's rewarding because it gives me a chance to thank the many people who helped me live my purpose and get this book out into the world, and difficult because I'm afraid of leaving someone out. So let me start by saying if you supported me in this process, I am very grateful.

I had some fantastic early inspiration from author and friend Tony Crabbe as well as coaching from Marcia Zina Mager, who served as an accountability partner to help me get my first draft written. This was complemented by encouragement from my family, Richard and Maddie, and transcriptions from Jenny Serra. Our team at Be Leadership shared knowledge and reflections on the social leadership skills that inspired me in my writing, and Patty Ryan worked tirelessly on referencing. Our brilliant Be Leadership interns Katie Kotler and McKenzie Lane analyzed and consolidated our secondary research and then supported the development of the book's individual and group exercises.

In the writing of this book, I had the chance to interview some incredibly inspiring social leaders from my network who serve as role models for me, and I'm thankful to them for their time and authenticity in those conversations. Additionally, several thought leaders gave me permission to reference their concepts, and I'd like to acknowledge this generosity:

- Larry Ackerman, for the use of his "what-I-love" activity (page 38).

- Jennifer Garvey Berger, for the use of her model that describes three ways of listening (page 74).

- Kate W. Isaacs from MIT Sloan School of Management, for the use of the Listening Challenge (page 88).

I benefited from partnering with Alain Dbjay and others from BNP Paribas on developing innovative social leadership programs and working with talent who actively participate in them, and I'm particularly grateful to those who allowed me to quote them here. Many thanks to my early readers, Sarah Rose, Mike Marquardt, Pieter Kooyman, Matt Smyth, and Peter Cauwelier, for the fantastic input that made this book stronger. Finally, I have benefited hugely from the talented team at Girl Friday Productions.

Thank you all.

Notes

INTRODUCTION

1   Personal conversation with Mary Klayder (2018).

CHAPTER 1: SOCIAL LEADERSHIP IN PRACTICE

Epigraph source: Jane Goodall (@ JaneGoodallInst), "'You cannot get through a single day without having an impact on the world around you. What you do makes a difference, and you have to decide what kind of difference you want to make.'—Dr. Jane Goodall, DBE, UN Messenger of Peace, Founder of the Jane Goodall Institute," Twitter, December 21, 2022, https://twitter.com/JaneGoodallInst/status/1605649830608572422

2   McKinsey & Company, "How COVID-19 Has Pushed Companies over the Technology Tipping Point—and Transformed Business Forever," Survey (October 5, 2020), n.p., https://www.mckinsey.com/capabilities/strategy-and-corporate-finance/our-insights/how-covid-19-has-pushed-companies-over-the-technology-tipping-point-and-transformed-business-forever

3   Mansoor Iqbal, "Zoom Revenue and Usage Statistics (2022)," Business of Apps (updated June 30, 2022), https://www.businessofapps.com/data/zoom-statistics/

4   Evan DeFilippis, Stephen Michael Impink, Madison Singell, Jeffrey T. Polzer, and Raffaella Sadun, "The Impact of COVID-19 on Digital Communication Patterns," Humanities and Social Sciences Communications (2022), n.p., https://papers.ssrn.com/sol3/papers.cfm?abstract_id=3654470

5   Chris Lilly, "Working from Home (WFH) Statistics," finder (updated February 4, 2022), n.p., https://www.finder.com/uk/working-from-home-statistics
See also: Francis Churchill, "Half Working from Home during Lockdown Are Unhappy with Work-Life Balance, Survey Finds," People Management (April 7, 2020), n.p., https://www.peoplemanagement.co.uk/news/articles/half-working-from-home-during-lockdown-unhappy-with-work-life-balance

6   Mayank Mohanti, "73% Employees Want Flexible Remote Work to Continue, Says Microsoft," India Times (March 23, 2021), n.p., https://www.indiatimes.com/technology/news/73-percent-employees-want-flexible-remote-work-microsoft-536878.html
See also: Microsoft, "More Than Half of UK Workers Would Consider Quitting Their Job If Hybrid Working Was Axed, Research Reveals," Microsoft News Centre UK (December 9, 2021), n.p., https://news.microsoft.com/en-gb/2021/12/09/more-than-half-of-uk-workers-would-consider-quitting-their-job-if-hybrid-working-was-axed-research-reveals/

7   Robert Waldinger, TEDx Beacon Talk (December 23, 2015), https://www.ted.com/talks/robert_waldinger_what_makes_a_good_life_lessons_from_the_longest_study_on_happiness
See also: Liz Mineo, "Good Genes Are Nice, but Joy Is Better," The Harvard Gazette (April 11, 2017), n.p., https://news.harvard.edu/gazette/story/2017/04/over-nearly-80-years-harvard-study-has-been-showing-how-to-live-a-healthy-and-happy-life

8   Culture Wizard, "Virtual Teams Survey: 2018 Executive Brief" (2018), n.p., https://cdn2.hubspot.net/hubfs/466336/Virtual%20Teams%20Survey-Executive%20Summary--Final%20(2018).pdf

9   Microsoft, "Great Expectations: Making Hybrid Work Work," Work Trend Index Annual Report (March 16, 2022), n.p., https://www.microsoft.com/en-us/worklab/work-trend-index/great-expectations-making-hybrid-work-work

10   Emily Kwong interviews Pragya Agarwal, "Understanding Unconscious Bias," NPR: Short Wave podcast (July 15, 2020), https://www.npr.org/2020/07/14 /891140598/understanding-unconscious -bias
See also: Nicole Martin, "How Much Data Is Collected Every Minute of the Day," *Forbes* (August 7, 2019), n.p., https://www.forbes .com/sites/nicolemartin1/2019/08/07/how -much-data-is-collected-every-minute-of -the-day/#40ecccfe3d66

11   Jack Loechner, "90% of Today's Data Created in Two Years," Media Post (December 22, 2016), n.p., https:// www.mediapost.com/publications /article/291358/90-of-todays-data-created -in-two-years.html

12   Jayanti, "OpenAI's ChatGPT Breaks User Adoption Rates to 1 Million," Analytics Insight (January 30, 2023), n.p., https:// www.analyticsinsight.net/openais-chatgpt -breaks-user-adoption-rates-to-1-million/

13   Krystal Hu, "ChatGPT Sets Record for Fastest-Growing User Base—Analyst Note," Reuters (February 2, 2023), n.p., https:// www.reuters.com/technology/chatgpt -sets-record-fastest-growing-user-base -analyst-note-2023-02-01/

14   World Economic Forum Report, "The Future of Jobs" (January 18, 2016), n.p., https://reports.weforum.org /future-of-jobs-2016/chapter-1-the -future-of-jobs-and-skills/

15   Personal interview with Chantal Peyre De Fabregues (March 2023).

16   Milton Friedman, "A Friedman Doctrine: The Social Responsibility of Business Is to Increase Its Profits," *New York Times Magazine* (September 13, 1970), n.p., https://www.nytimes.com/1970/09/13 /archives/a-friedman-doctrine-the-social -responsibility-of-business-is-to.html

17   Michael E. Porter and Mark R. Kramer, "Creating Shared Value," *Harvard Business Review Magazine* (January–February 2011),

n.p., https://hbr.org/2011/01/the-big -idea-creating-shared-value

18   John Kotter and James Heskett, "Why Business Must Harness the Power of Purpose," Ernst and Young Global (December 15, 2020), n.p., https://www .ey.com/en_gl/purpose/why-business -must-harness-the-power-of-purpose

19   Governance & Accountability Institute Research Results, "86% of S&P 500 Index® Companies Publish Sustainability / Responsibility Reports in 2018" (May 17, 2019), n.p., https://www .sustainability-reports.com/86-of-sp-500 -index-companies-publish-sustainability -responsibility-reports-in-2018/

20   Governance & Accountability Institute, "All-Time High of Sustainability Reports among U.S. Publicly-Traded Companies: 96% of S&P 500 and 81% of Russell 1000" (2022), n.p., https://www.ga-institute .com/research/ga-research-directory /sustainability-reporting-trends/2022 -sustainability-reporting-in-focus/

21   Arne Gast, Pablo Illanes, Nina Probst, Bill Schaninger, and Bruce Simpson, "Purpose: Shifting from Why to How," *McKinsey & Company Quarterly* (April 22, 2020), n.p., https://www .mckinsey.com/capabilities/people-and -organizational-performance/our-insights /purpose-shifting-from-why-to-how

22   The British Academy, "Principles for Purposeful Business" (2019), n.p., https://www.thebritishacademy.ac.uk /publications/future-of-the-corporation -principles-for-purposeful-business/

23   Deloitte Brandvoice, "For Millennials and Gen Zs, Social Issues Are Top of Mind: Here's How Organizations Can Drive Meaningful Change," *Forbes* (July 22, 2021), n.p., https://www.forbes.com/sites /deloitte/2021/07/22/for-millennials-and -gen-zs-social-issues-are-top-of-mind -heres-how-organizations-can-drive -meaningful-change/?sh=74748a53450c

See also: Elena Chatzopoulou and Adrian de Kiewiet, "Millennials' Evaluation of Corporate Social Responsibility: The Wants and Needs of the Largest and Most Ethical Generation," *Journal of Consumer Behavior*, Vol. 20, No. 3, https://doi.org/10.1002/cb.1882

24 "The Business Case for Purpose," *Harvard Business Review*, sponsored by Ernst & Young (2020), n.p., https://assets.ey.com/content/dam/ey-sites/ey-com/en_gl/topics/digital/ey-the-business-case-for-purpose.pdf

25 Personal interview with Vlada Bortnik (February 2023).

CHAPTER 2: EXPLORING YOUR REASON TO BE

Epigraph source: Dolly Parton (@DollyParton), "'Find out who you are and do it on purpose,'" Twitter, July 20, 2009, https://twitter.com/DollyParton/status/2740290248

26 "One Third of Your Life Is Spent at Work," Gettysburg College, https://www.gettysburg.edu/news/stories?id=79db7b34-630c-4f49-ad32-4ab9ea48e72b&pageTitle=1%2F3+of+your+life+is+spent+at+work

27 James Kerr, "Legacy: Lessons on Winning at Life from the All Blacks, the World's Most Successful Sporting Team," *Constable & Robinson*, London (December 17, 2013), 36.

28 Emily Esfahani Smith, *The Power of Meaning: Crafting a Life That Matters*, New York, Crown (January 10, 2017), 85–86.
See also: Majid Fotuhi and Sara Mehr, "The Science behind the Powerful Benefits of Having a Purpose," *Practical Neurology* (September 2015), n.p.
See also: Marie Earvolino-Ramirez, "Resilience: A Concept Analysis," *Nursing Forum*, Vol. 42, No. 2 (April–June 2007), https://nursingacademy.com/wp-content/uploads/2020/01/resilienceaconceptanalysis.pdf

29 Naina Dhingra, Andrew Samo, Bill Schaninger, and Matt Schrimper, "Help Your Employees Find Purpose—or Watch Them Leave," McKinsey (April 5, 2021), https://www.mckinsey.com/capabilities/people-and-organizational-performance/our-insights/help-your-employees-find-purpose-or-watch-them-leave

30 Dhruv Khullar, "Finding Purpose for a Good Life. But Also a Healthy One," The Upshot, *New York Times* (January 1, 2018), n.p., https://www.nytimes.com/2018/01/01/upshot/finding-purpose-for-a-good-life-but-also-a-healthy-one.html

31 Nick Craig and Scott A. Snook, "From Purpose to Impact," *Harvard Business Review Magazine* (May 2014), n.p., https://hbr.org/2014/05/from-purpose-to-impact

32 J. P. Flaum, "When It Comes to Business Leadership, Nice Guys Finish First," Green Peak Partners with Cornell University (September 2018), n.p., https://greenpeakpartners.com/wp-content/uploads/2018/09/Green-Peak_Cornell-University-Study_What-predicts-success.pdf

33 Anna Sutton, Helen Williams, and Christopher Allinson, "A Longitudinal, Mixed Method Evaluation of Self-Awareness Training in the Workplace," *European Journal of Training and Development* (2015).

34 Thomas Merton, *Thoughts in Solitude*, USA, Farrar, Straus and Cudahy (1958), 22.

35 Larry Ackerman, *The Identity Code: The 8 Essential Questions for Finding Your Purpose and Place in the World*, Random House (December 27, 2005), n.p.

36 Personal interview with Chantal Peyre De Fabregues (March 2023).

37 "Complete Our Self-Assessment. Become a Social Leader," Be Leadership,

https://be-leadership.com/personal -assessment

38   Simon Sinek, David Mead, and Peter Docker, *Find Your Why: A Practical Guide for Discovering Purpose for You and Your Team*, Brentford, UK, Portfolio (September 5, 2017), 37.

CHAPTER 3: LEADING WITH COURAGEOUS AUTHENTICITY

Epigraph source: Susan David, "The Emotional Agility Manifesto," Susan David, August 17, 2022, https:// www.susandavid.com/newsletter /the-emotional-agility-manifesto/

39   Brené Brown, *Atlas of the Heart: Mapping Meaningful Connection and the Language of Human Experience*, New York, Random House Publishing Group (November 30, 2021), 155.

40   Stephen Joseph, *Authentic: How to Be Yourself and Why It Matters*, London, Piatkus, (2016), 27.

41   Personal interview with Bayile Adeoti (September 2022).

42   Ron Friedman, "5 Things High-Performing Teams Do Differently," *Harvard Business Review* (October 21, 2021), n.p., https://hbr.org/2021/10/5-things-high -performing-teams-do-differently

43   Brené Brown, *Daring Greatly: How the Courage to Be Vulnerable Transforms the Way We Live, Love, Parent, and Lead*, New York, Penguin Publishing Group (September 11, 2012), n.p.

44   Personal interview with Jean-Philippe Courtois (February 2023).

45   Drake Baer, "Mark Zuckerberg Explains Why Facebook Doesn't 'Move Fast and Break Things' Anymore," *Business Insider* (May 2, 2014), n.p., https://www .businessinsider.com/mark-zuckerberg-on -facebooks-new-motto-2014-5?r=US&IR=T

46   Ed Catmull and Amy Wallace, *Creativity, Inc.*, New York, Random House (April 8, 2014), Kindle Version, location 1670.

47   Personal interview with Bryan Nixon (September 2022).

48   Malala Yousafzai, Women of the World Conference, London, 2014.

49   Winston Churchill quote, Dan Steinber, "RGIII and Winston Churchill," *Washington Post* (October 24, 2014), n.p., https://www .washingtonpost.com/news/dc-sports-bog /wp/2014/10/24/rgiii-and-winston-churchill

50   Jim Detert, *Choosing Courage: The Everyday Guide to Being Brave at Work*, Boston, Harvard Business Review Press (May 18, 2021).

51   Karissa Thacker, *The Art of Authenticity: Tools to Become an Authentic Leader and Your Best Self*, New York, Wiley (March 7, 2016), 140.

CHAPTER 4: ADOPTING A BEGINNER'S MINDSET

Epigraph source: Bianca Bosker, "Cisco Tech Chief Outlines the Advantages of Being a Woman in Tech," HuffPost, October 27, 2011, https://www.huffingtonpost.co.uk /entry/cisco-chief-technology-officer -woman-in-tech_n_1035880

52   Albert Einstein letter to Carl Seeling (March 11, 1952), Einstein Archive 39–013.

53   Warren Berger, "Einstein and Questioning: Exploring the Inquiring Mind of One of Our Greatest Thinkers," *A More Beautiful Question (blog)*, n.p., https:// amorebeautifulquestion.com /einstein-questioning/

54   Personal conversation with Michael Marquardt (2008).

55   Shunryū Suzuki, *Zen Mind, Beginner's Mind: Informal Talks on Zen Meditation and Practice*, New York, Weatherhill (1970), 1.

56   Personal interview with Anita Bhasin (October 2022).

57 Personal interview with Peter Muthaura (November 2022).

58 Jennifer Garvey Berger, *Unlocking Leadership Mindtraps: How to Thrive in Complexity*, Redwood City, Stanford City Press (2019).

59 Berger, *Unlocking Leadership Mindtraps*, 51–57.

60 Carol S. Dweck, *Mindset: The New Psychology of Success, How We Can Learn to Fulfill Our Potential*, New York, Random House (2006).

61 Personal interview with Bryan Nixon (September 2022).

62 Personal interview with Jean-Philippe Courtois (February 2023).

63 Personal conversation with Richard Strudwick (2022).

64 Brian Grazer as told to Margy Rochlin, "Curiosity Thrills This Cat," *AARP: The Magazine* (August/September 2015), n.p., https://www.aarp.org /entertainment/television/info-2015 /brian-grazer-celeb-news/

65 Adam Grant, *Think Again: The Power of Knowing What You Don't Know*, New York, Penguin Publishing Group (February 2, 2021), 257.

CHAPTER 5: HARNESSING DIVERSE THINKING

Epigraph source: African proverb

66 Sundiatu Dixon-Fyle and Sara Prince, *Diversity Wins: How Inclusion Matters*, McKinsey & Company (May 19, 2020), n.p., https://www.mckinsey.com /featured-insights/diversity-and-inclusion /diversity-wins-how-inclusion-matters

67 Richard L. Zweigenhaft, "Diversity among Fortune 500 CEOs from 2000 to 2020: White Women, Hi-Tech South Asians, and Economically Privileged Multilingual Immigrants from Around the World," Who Rules American Blog, University of California at Santa Cruz Sociology Department (January 2021), n.p., https://whorulesamerica.ucsc.edu/power /diversity_update_2020.html

68 BoardEx, "Global Gender Diversity 2022," Altrata (July 28, 2022), n.p., https://altrata.com/reports/global -gender-diversity-2022/

69 Julie S. Nugent, Alixandra Pollack, and Dnika J. Travis, "The Day-to-Day Experiences of Workplace Inclusion and Exclusion," *Catalyst* (September 29, 2016), n.p., https://www.catalyst.org/wp-content /uploads/2019/01/the_day_to_day _experiences_of_workplace_inclusion _and_exclusion.pdf

70 Brené Brown, *Braving the Wilderness: The Quest for True Belonging and the Courage to Stand Alone*, New York, Random House Publishing Group (September 12, 2017), 63.

71 Emily Kubin and Christian von Sikorski, "The Role of (Social) Media in Political Polarization: A Systematic Review," Annals of the International Communication Association, Informa UK Limited, trading as Taylor & Francis Group (2021), n.p., https:// www.tandfonline.com/doi/pdf/10.1080/238 08985.2021.1976070

72 Fox News Poll of 1,003 American registered voters during April 28–May 1, 2022 (May 3, 2022), n.p., https:// static.foxnews.com/foxnews.com /content/uploads/2022/05/Fox_April-28 -May-1-2022_National_Topline_May-3 -Release.pdf

73 Geoffrey Skelley and Holly Fuong, "3 in 10 Americans Name Political Polarization as a Top Issue Facing the Country," FiveThirtyEight, Caviness & Cates Communities (June 14, 2022), n.p., https:// fivethirtyeight.com/features/3-in-10 -americans-named-political-polarization -as-a-top-issue-facing-the-country/

74 Fernando Casal Bertoa and Jose Rama, "Polarizations: What Do We Know and What Can We Do about It?" Frontiers

Political Science (June 20, 2021), n.p., https://www.frontiersin.org/articles/10.3389/fpos.2021.687695/full

75   Ursula K. Le Guin, "Telling Is Listening," in *The Wave in the Mind: Talks and Essays on the Writer, the Reader, and the Imagination*, Boulder, CO, Shambhala Publications (February 17, 2004), 196.

76   The Listening Challenge, "Do You Have the Courage to Hear the Whole Story?" (2021), n.p., https://www.listeningchallenge.org/

77   Kate Isaacs and Kara Penn, "Red Fathers and Blue Daughters Bridging the Political Divide," Medium (July 2022), https://medium.com/@kateisaacs/red-fathers-and-blue-daughters-bridging-the-political-divide-62f461000343
See also: Meredith Somers, "This 4-Step 'Listening Challenge' Can Help Reduce Polarized Discourse," MIT Management, Sloan School (August 2, 2022), n.p., https://mitsloan.mit.edu/ideas-made-to-matter/4-step-listening-challenge-can-help-reduce-polarized-discourse

78   David Epstein, *Range: Why Generalists Triumph in a Specialized World*, New York, Penguin Publishing Group (May 28, 2019).

79   Personal interview with Bryan Nixon (September 2022).

80   Amos Tversky and Daniel Kahneman, "Judgement under Uncertainty: Heuristics and Biases," *Science*, American Association for the Advancement of Science, New Series, Vol. 185, No. 4157 (September 27, 1974), 1124–1131, https://www2.psych.ubc.ca/~schaller/Psyc590Readings/TverskyKahneman1974.pdf

81   Daniel Kahneman, *Thinking, Fast and Slow*, Penguin (May 10, 2012), n.p.

82   Brian Rene Morrissette, "Cognitive Bias Codex," Wikipedia Commons (November 29 2017), https://upload.wikimedia.org/wikipedia/commons/c/ce/Cognitive_Bias_Codex_With_Definitions%2C

_an_Extension_of_the_work_of_John_Manoogian_by_Brian_Morrissette.jpg

83   The Human Library, Denmark (founded in 2000), n.p., https://humanlibrary.org/

84   Chimamanda Ngozi Adichie, "The Danger of a Single Story," TEDGlobal (2009), n.p., https://www.ted.com/talks/chimamanda_ngozi_adichie_the_danger_of_a_single_story?language=en

85   Liza A. Talusan, "Practicing Inclusion: Icebreakers and Team Builders for Diversity," Office of Intercultural Affairs, Stonehill College (July 20, 2012), n.p., https://studentlife.mit.edu/sites/default/files/Diversity-based%20Teambuilders%20and%20Icebreakers%20from%20Stonehill%20College.pdf

86   Personal interview with Stephanie Parry (June 2021).

87   Scott E. Page, *The Diversity Bonus: How Great Teams Pay Off in the Knowledge Economy (Our Compelling Interests, 2)* Princeton, Princeton University Press and the Andrew Mellon Foundation (September 19, 2017), n.p.

88   Adam Grant, "You're More Likely to Get a Job through Weaker Ties," *Video, Inc. Magazine* (February 20, 2015), https://www.youtube.com/watch?v=sW-hg2bcqUE

CHAPTER 6: BUILDING TEAMS THAT TALK

Epigraph source: Aaron Hurst, "How Denise Morrison Took Processed Food Icon Campbell's on a Fresh Food Buying Spree," Fast Company, March 2, 2017, https://www.fastcompany.com/3068634/how-denise-morrison-took-processed-food-icon-campbells-on-a-fresh-food-bu

89   Michael Chui, James Manyika, Jacques Bughin, Richard Dobbs, Charles Roxburgh, Hugo Sarrazin, Geoffrey Sands, and Magdalena Westergren, "The Social Economy: Unlocking Value and Productivity through Social Technologies," McKinsey

Global Institute (July 1, 2012), n.p., https://www.mckinsey.com/industries/technology-media-and-telecommunications/our-insights/the-social-economy

90 Jessica Rohman, "The Business Case for High Trust Culture," *Great Place to Work* (2016), n.p., https://s3.amazonaws.com/media.greatplacetowork.com/pdfs/Business+Case+for+a+High-Trust+Culture_081816.pdf

91 "Frederick W. Taylor, American Inventor and Engineer," *Britannica*, n.p., https://www.britannica.com/biography/Frederick-W-Taylor

92 Boris Groysberg and Michael Slind, *Talk, Inc.: How Trusted Leaders Use Conversation to Power Their Organizations*, Boston, Harvard Business Review Press (June 19, 2012), 25.

93 Jim Whitehurst and Gary Hamel, "The Open Organization: Igniting Passion and Performance," *Harvard Business Review Press*, Boston (May 12, 2015), 156.

94 Whitehurst and Hamel, "The Open Organization," 154.

95 Groysberg and Slind, *Talk, Inc.* 4.

96 Groysberg and Slind, *Talk, Inc.* 4.

97 Ed Catmull and Amy Wallace, *Creativity Inc.*, New York, Random House (April 8, 2014), Kindle Version, location 1374.

98 Personal interview with Bryan Nixon (September 2022).

99 Groysberg and Slind, *Talk, Inc.*, 173–75.

100 Personal interview with Bryan Nixon (September 2022).

101 Presentation by Angela McKenna, Salesforce, at the Global Conference of the World Institute for Action Learning (2022).

102 McKenna, Salesforce (2022).

103 Mary Mesaglio, "4 Actions to Be a Strong Leader during COVID-19 Disruption," *Gartner* (November 18, 2020), n.p., https://www.gartner.com/smarterwithgartner/4-actions-to-be-a-good-leader-during-covid-19-disruption

CHAPTER 7: FOCUSING ON ACCOUNTABILITY

Epigraph source: OWN, "Oprah on Taking Responsibility for Your Life," YouTube, October 21, 2011, https://www.youtube.com/watch?v=Dp_cmLfJZ1w

104 Adrian F. Ward, Kristen Duke, Ayelet Gneezy, and Maarten W. Bos, "Brain Drain: The Mere Presence of One's Own Smartphone Reduces Available Cognitive Capacity," McCombs School of Business, University of Texas News (June 26, 2017), n.p., https://news.utexas.edu/2017/06/26/the-mere-presence-of-your-smartphone-reduces-brain-power/

105 Stephen Covey, *The 7 Habits of Highly Effective People*, London, Simon & Schuster (2020), n.p.

106 "Address at the Second Assembly of the World Council of Churches, Evanston, Illinois" (August 19, 1954), American Presidency Project, https://www.presidency.ucsb.edu/documents/address-the-second-assembly-the-world-council-churches-evanston-illinois

107 Jackie Yeaney, "Power of Daily Guideposts," LinkedIn (June 10, 2022), n.p., https://www.linkedin.com/pulse/power-daily-guideposts-jackie-yeaney/?trackingId=NKifB3ZNSVmwAyJklOWrOw%3D%3D

108 Meredith Smith, "How Jackie Yeaney Made Peace with 'Imposter Syndrome'," Ideas Made to Matter, The Bias Cut, MIT Sloan School of Management (December 13, 2022), n.p., https://mitsloan.mit.edu/ideas-made-to-matter/how-jackie-yeaney-made-peace-imposter-syndrome

109 Juliet Funt, "A Minute to Think: Reclaim Creativity, Conquer Busyness, and Do Your Best Work," New York, *Harper Business* (August 3, 2021), n.p.

110 Fred Kofman, *Conscious Business: How*

to *Build Value through Values*, Louisville, CO, Sounds True (January 1, 1994), n.p.

111 The Smiley Group: State of the Black Union 2007, Afternoon Session, C-Span. org, "Bruce Gordon Accountability Ladder," video clip from 1:38:26–1:43:46 (February 11, 2007).

CHAPTER 8: LEADING BY EXAMPLE

Epigraph source: Michelle Obama, "Transcript: Michelle Obama's Convention Speech," NPR, Speech to the Democratic National Convention in North Carolina, September 4, 2012, https://www.npr .org/2012/09/04/160578836/transcript -michelle-obamas-convention-speech

112 Mark Horwitch and Meredith Whipple Callahan, "How Leaders Inspire: Cracking the Code: Bain Research Identified 33 Distinct and Tangible Attributes That Are Statistically Significant in Creating Inspiration in Others," Bain & Company (June 09, 2016), n.p., https:// www.bain.com/insights/how-leaders -inspire-cracking-the-code/

113 Jim Harter, "Employee Engagement vs. Employee Satisfaction and Organizational Culture," Workplace, Gallup (April 12, 2017), n.p., https://www.gallup.com/workplace /236366/right-culture-not-employee -satisfaction.aspx

114 Taylor Branch, *Parting the Waters: America in the King Years, 1954–63*, Simon & Shuster (November 15, 1989), 875–876, 881–882.

115 Personal interview with Jean-Philippe Courtois (February 2023).

116 John Medina, *Brain Rules: 12 Principles for Surviving and Thriving at Work, Home, and School*, Pear Press (2014), 106–107.

117 Lisa VeneKlasen and Valerie Miller, "Power and Empowerment," in *A New Weave of Power, People & Politics: The Action Guide for Advocacy and Citizen Participation*, Warwickshire, Practical Action Publishing

(August 4, 2007), 7, https://justassociates .org/en/resources/new-weave-power -people-politics-action-guide-advocacy -and-citizen-participation
See also: Raji Hunjan and Soumountha Keophilavong, "Power and Making Change Happen," Carnegie UK Trust (2010), 15–17, https://www.carnegieuktrust .org.uk/publications/power-and-making -change-happen/

118 HarperCollins, "Empower," Collins Dictionary (2023), https://www .collinsdictionary.com/dictionary /english/empower

119 Personal interview with Katie Kotler (September 2022).

120 Michael Marquardt, Shannon Banks, Peter Cauwelier, and Choon Seng Ng, *Optimizing the Power of Action Learning: Real-Time Strategies for Developing Leaders, Building Teams and Transforming Organizations*. Boston, Nicholas Brealey (2018).

121 James W. Moore, "What Is the Sense of Agency and Why Does it Matter?," *Frontiers in Psychology*, Vol. 7 (August 29, 2016), https://doi.org/10.3389/fpsyg.2016.01272

122 Personal interview with Jean-Philippe Courtois (February 2023).

123 Adam Grant, "Are You a Giver or a Taker?," TED@IBM (January 3, 2017), n.p., https://www.ted.com/talks/adam_grant _are_you_a_giver_or_a_taker/transcript

124 Personal interview with Vlada Bortnik (February 2023).

125 Adam Rifkin, "How a (Very) Little, Daily Favor Can Change Your Life," Huff Post (September 3, 2013), n.p., https://www .huffpost.com/entry/five-minute-favor -adam-rifkin_n_3805090

126 Ashley V. Whillans, Elizabeth W. Dunn, Gillian M. Sandstrom, Sally S. Dickerson, and Kenneth M. Madden, "Is Spending Money on Others Good for Your Heart?," *Health Psychology*, American Psychological

Association, Vol. 35, No. 6 (2016), 574–583, https://www.hbs.edu/ris/Publication%20Files/1526_30511abd-038c-45c6-adcc-90285f6bd629.pdf
See also: S. Han, K. Kim, and J. A. Burr, "Stress-Buffering Effects of Volunteering on Salivary Cortisol: Results from a Daily Diary Study," National Institutes of Health, National Library of Medicine (online, November 11, 2018), n.p., https://www.ncbi.nlm.nih.gov/pmc/articles/PMC6228389/
See also: Doug Oman, Carl E. Thorensen, and Kay McMahon, "Volunteerism and Morality among the Community-Dwelling Elderly," *Sage Journals*, Vol. 4, No. 3 (May 1999), n.p., https://journals.sagepub.com/doi/abs/10.1177/135910539900400301

127 Adam Grant, *Give and Take: A Revolutionary Approach to Success*, Penguin Publishing Group (April 9, 2013).

CHAPTER 9: BUILDING YOUR LEADERSHIP BRAND

Epigraph source: Larry Ackerman, author of *The Identity Code*

128 Patagonia, "Patagonia's Next Chapter: Earth Is Now Our Only Shareholder," Patagonia Works (September 14, 2022), n.p., https://www.patagoniaworks.com/press/2022/9/14/patagonias-next-chapter-earth-is-now-our-only-shareholder

129 World Economic Forum in collaboration with Martin Armstrong, Statista, "Company Given Away to Support the Fight in Saving Our Planet and Tackle the Climate Crisis" (September 23, 2022), n.p., https://www.weforum.org/agenda/2022/09/the-size-company-given-away-to-save-the-planet-earth/

130 Daniel Schwabel, "Personal Branding Interview: Robert Kiyosaki," Personal Branding Blog (November 8, 2009), n.p., https://www.personalbrandingblog.com/personal-branding-interview-robert-kiyosaki/

131 Simon Sinek, David Mead, and Peter Docker, *Find Your Why: A Practical Guide for Discovering Purpose for You and Your Team*, Brentford, UK, Portfolio (September 5, 2017), 37.

132 Brother David Steindl-Rast, *Gratefulness, the Heart of Prayer: An Approach to Life in Fullness*, Mahwah, New Jersey, Paulist Press (1984), 192.

About the Author

Shannon Banks is managing director of Be Leadership and an award-winning facilitator, consultant, and coach. A pioneer in the field of social leadership, she founded her company in 2014 to help organizations bring their purpose to life through their people. Shannon has delivered quality, bespoke work to diverse clients across many sectors, including Roche, BNP Paribas, and the UK House of Commons, and has partnered with world-changing organizations such as Teach for India, Grameen Foundation, and Siel Bleu.

Shannon spent twenty years in the technology industry, including seventeen years at Microsoft, where she held a variety of global leadership roles across the business and HR. She has won international awards for her work in leadership development and talent management and is a sought-after public speaker.

Shannon was the first Action Learning coach certified in the United Kingdom by the World Institute for Action Learning (WIAL). As one of only twenty coaches globally to obtain the Master Action Learning Coach qualification, Shannon frequently teaches the Action Learning Coach Certification courses held in Britain and uses Action Learning to support her clients in creating sustainable cultural change. She is coauthor of the third edition of the field-defining book *Optimizing the Power of Action Learning*.

Shannon lives outside of London with her husband and daughter. She is a slow but persistent runner and avid reader who enjoys painting watercolors and spending time in her vegetable garden. She is active in her local community and volunteers with the Runnymede Foodbank. You can find her online at shannonbanksauthor.com.